Davis & Elkins College
GRATEFULLY ACKNOWLEDGES

John Harling, Class of 1953, Trustee

Davis Trust Company

FOR THEIR GENEROUS SUPPORT
OF THIS PROJECT.

CHAD
WAGNER '94

Davis & Elkins COLLEGE

One Hundred Years
Honoring Our Traditions
Celebrating Our Future

David R. Turner

PUBLISHED BY WDG PUBLISHING

Davis&Elkins COLLEGE

One Hundred Years
Honoring Our Traditions
Celebrating Our Future

David R. Turner

Frontispiece: The Arcade, walkway arches between Liberal Arts and Albert Halls

PUBLISHED BY WDG PUBLISHING

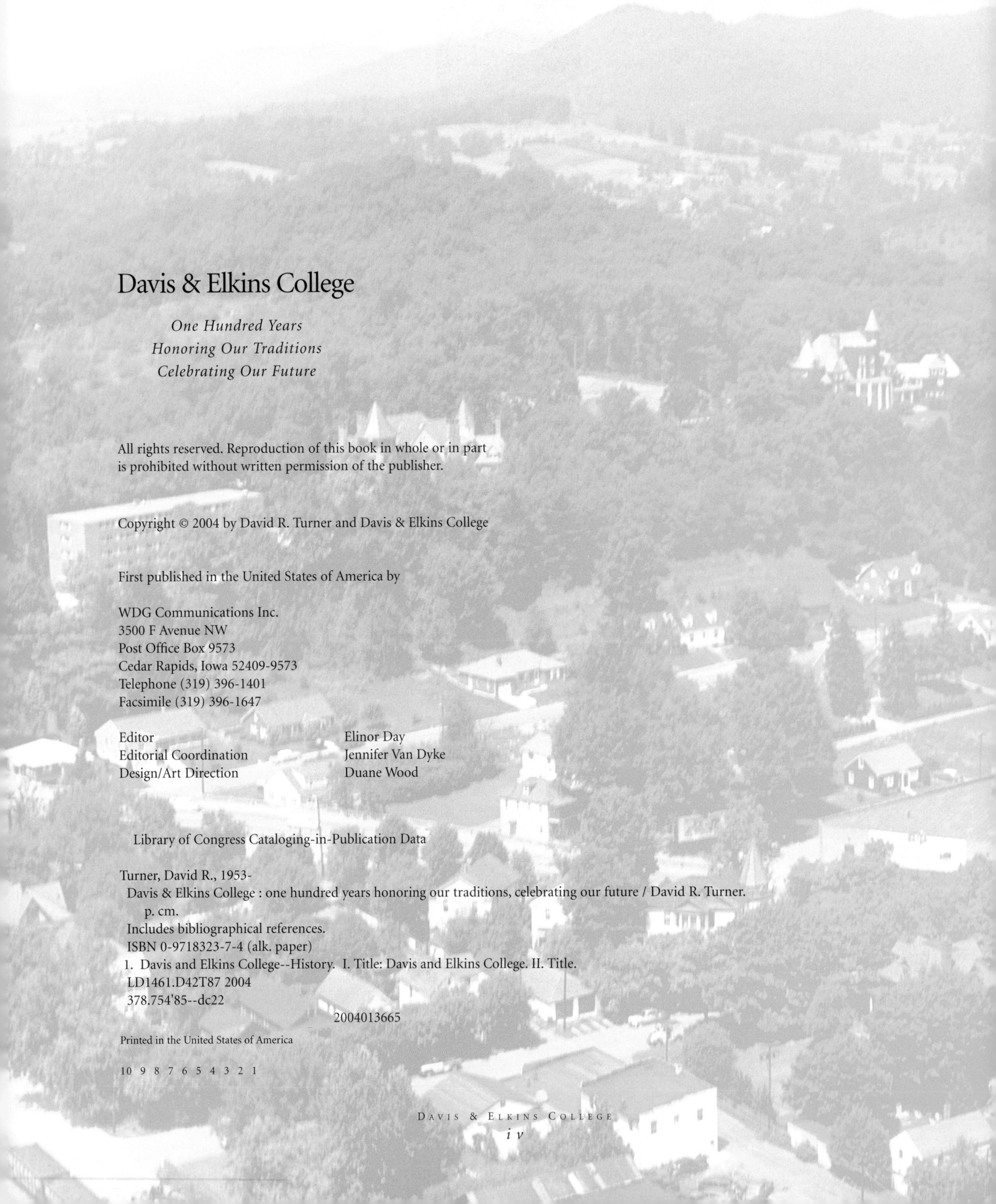

Davis & Elkins College

One Hundred Years
Honoring Our Traditions
Celebrating Our Future

First published in the United States of America by

WDG Communications Inc.
3500 F Avenue NW
Post Office Box 9573
Cedar Rapids, Iowa 52409-9573
Telephone (319) 396-1401
Facsimile (319) 396-1647

Editor   Elinor Day
Editorial Coordination   Jennifer Van Dyke
Design/Art Direction   Duane Wood

   Library of Congress Cataloging-in-Publication Data

Turner, David R., 1953-
  Davis & Elkins College : one hundred years honoring our traditions, celebrating our future / David R. Turner.
     p. cm.
  Includes bibliographical references.
  ISBN 0-9718323-7-4 (alk. paper)
  1. Davis and Elkins College--History. I. Title: Davis and Elkins College. II. Title.
  LD1461.D42T87 2004
  378.754'85--dc22

                    2004013665

Printed in the United States of America

10 9 8 7 6 5 4 3 2 1

Table of Contents

Introduction
D&E, One Hundred Years

Page *vi*

A Brief History of
Davis & Elkins College

Page 1

Athletics at
Davis & Elkins College

Page 25

Davis & Elkins College
Gallery

Page 40

Service First:
Faculty and Staff

Page 59

Student Life

Page 79

Epilogue

Page 102

Bibliography
Acknowledgements

Page 104

1904 · CENTENNIAL · 2004

v

1922-1923 Faculty (seated, from left) Vice President and Professor of History and English Dr. Willis H. Wilcox, Professor of Physics and Civil Engineering Charles Albert, President James E. Allen, Professor of Politics, Social Sciences and Philosophy Thomas J. Hale, Mrs. Willis H. Wilcox, Professor of Instrumental Music; (standing, from left) Mrs. Geneva Adams Metzler, Professor of Expression and Dramatic Arts, Miss Nell Keim, Professor of Commercial Subjects, Mrs. Lillian Davidson, Professor of Vocal Music, Miss Virgie Harris, Registrar, Librarian and Professor of Spanish, Professor of Science, H.G. Ross, Mrs. Charlotte Pekary, Professor of Modern Languages, Professor of Mathematics Harry Whetsell, Instructor, Athletic Director and Head Coach Richard Hamill, Dr. Helen M. Clarke, Professor of Education

D&E, One Hundred Years

During the fall semester of the 1999-2000 academic year, a new mission statement appeared in the catalogue of Davis & Elkins College. It stated that the college "offers a personalized undergraduate education firmly rooted in the liberal arts tradition that values breadth and depth of learning and affirms the importance of tradition and experimentation...." Five years from its second century, Davis & Elkins was sharpening its purposes and clarifying its goals.

On April 16, 1999, Thomas Mann, in his inaugural address as twelfth president of the college, issued the call for change, fully honoring the traditions that Davis & Elkins had nurtured in the past. In this inaugural address, Mann not only re-stated the academic goals of the mission statement, he reaffirmed D&E's commitment to the local and world communities.

Furthermore, he stated that the college should "renew our acquaintance with the vision that motivated United States Senators Henry Gassaway Davis and Stephen Benton Elkins." He lauded the college for being innovative and embracing "individuality while nurturing diversity." More importantly, Mann emphasized the need for change, framed within the context of its past. But he warned against a sentimental interpretation of history, declaring that "nostalgia is a poor—a very poor—foundation upon which to build a small, private liberal arts college."

He urged his listeners to work for a college that would help meet the needs of a technologically ever more complicated society in the 21st century. Mann admitted that to embrace the new while tapping the wisdom of the past was a complicated task, one that must be faced with subtlety and purpose.

Although Mann had been associated with the college for less than a year, he demonstrated that he fully grasped the history of the institution. Throughout its history, D&E has not so much reinvented itself as adjusted to changing times. All the while, it has stayed on course even if it was required to zig and zag from time to time. Despite changes, D&E has remained true to its mission; indeed, change has been part of its tradition since 1904.

This illustrated history is an attempt to examine the college's past in a series of essays. It does not attempt to duplicate the superb efforts of Thomas Richard Ross in his seventy-five-year commemorative. Indeed, his study provides a cornerstone for this more modest effort. This centennial history represents an attempt to place the college in perspective rather than provide a chronicle of events. The illustrations offer a visual perspective that words can sometimes not improve upon.

Writing this retrospective has been an enormously rewarding task, and one that could not have been done without considerable help. I thank, particularly, Thomas Richard Ross for his instructive comments, as well as Gloria Payne and Beth Kittle for sharing their perspectives on the college. Pat Schumann, vice president for college advancement, helped enormously by providing some primary sources. Library Director Ellis Hodgin freely offered his services, and Peter Okun, my colleague from the English Department, offered encouragement and support. In addition, Robin Price in the president's office provided documents with characteristic efficiency, and, finally, Jean Jones, who typed and proofed the work, helped spare me from some errors. All have been helpful, but mistakes can be laid directly at my door.

David R. Turner, Ph.D.

Chair, Department of History and Political Science
Thomas Richard Ross Professor of History and the Humanities

A Brief History of Davis & Elkins College

Henry Gassaway Davis seemed as surprised as everyone else when he heard that he had been chosen as the Democratic nominee for Vice President in 1904. An octogenarian, Davis's selection was widely regarded as a not-too-well-disguised attempt to exploit his vast financial resources for the upcoming campaign. As Davis himself wryly observed, the party "just wanted to tap my barrel" in a long-shot effort to unseat President Theodore Roosevelt. To Henry Cabot Lodge, a close friend of TR, it appeared positively bizarre "to nominate a man eighty-one years old," but he figured that "it means money and a desperate bid for West Virginia."

Opposite: Senator Henry Gassaway Davis

Yet, if the Democratic Party expected an avalanche of cash, they badly misjudged their man. Davis, a shrewd businessman, had no intention of being a financial front for an enterprise that seemed doomed from the start. Judge Alton Parker of New York, the presidential nominee, represented the highly unpopular faction of the party allied with former President Grover Cleveland. Even William Jennings Bryan, the Democratic standard-bearer in 1896 and 1900, adjudged the waters as too choppy and too cold in 1904 and eschewed a race against the enormously popular Roosevelt. Given TR's intervention in the Northern Securities Case and the Anthracite Coal Strike in 1902, some Democrats believed they could attack the president on his conservative flank. It was a strategy fraught with folly. Despite misgivings and their displeasure with Roosevelt's assault on monopoly and big coal, conservatives lined up behind the Republican ticket. George Cortelyou, Roosevelt's campaign chairman, vigorously tapped the barrels of America's corporate elites. The nomination of Davis, first thought of as a means to hook a lucrative asset, proved an ineffective strategy.

It has been a standard piece of American political lore that Davis contributed next to nothing in 1904—a charge recently made in a biography of President John Kennedy (although Davis was incorrectly named as Bryan's nominee in 1908). Actually he spent close to $140,000 of his own money, much of it in West Virginia. Davis, whose political motto was "charity begins at home," protected his interests in West Virginia. He had no intention of being milked by the Democratic Party of a huge fortune in order to do the impossible, namely, defeat a popular incumbent. As usually was the case in a long and successful career in business and politics, Davis's instincts did not fail him. Not only did Roosevelt take 57 percent of the vote, he captured West Virginia by a sizeable majority.

The campaign in 1904 displayed Davis's lifelong affinity for prudence. It was not that he wanted to appear ungrateful for the honor the Democrats had bestowed on him; he merely proved that he was no fool. It might have been Parker's campaign, but it was surely Davis's money to be doled out in a manner he saw fit. This baronial and conservative attitude displayed itself in an entirely different project completed on September 21, 1904. A college named for Davis and his son-in-law Stephen Benton Elkins was dedicated in Elkins, West Virginia. The ceremonies were the completion of a more-than-a-decade effort to found a college in North Central West Virginia. Of the two, Davis placed more of his personal imprimatur on the institution. His decisions would affect the college for years to come. During its infancy, Davis & Elkins would bear the marks of a courtly and cautious albeit generous conservative, who had no desire to throw good money after bad.

This close-to-the-vest approach reflected the habits of a lifetime. As with Andrew Carnegie, who became a personal friend of Davis, the future Senator of West Virginia worked his way up, beginning his career as a humble brakeman for the Baltimore and Ohio Railway. Enamored of the idea that opportunities were presented but that success was earned, Davis, as did Abraham Lincoln, started as an admirer of the Whig leader Henry Clay of Kentucky. Carefully working himself to the top, Davis later accumulated vast wealth, first in the railroad industry and later in timber and coal. By 1904, Davis had become the wealthiest man in West Virginia. Political power had come in the wake of this financial success. In 1871, he became a senator in the relatively new state of West Virginia. As a senator, he became one of the most ardent advocates of a high protective tariff, which shielded industrialists like himself from the perceived evils of free trade. His conservative instincts aside, he also had a

strong philanthropic streak, but this, too, came with a heavy dose of caution that would govern his decisions regarding Davis & Elkins College.

Although Davis anxiously desired to establish a college in Elkins that would rival prominent schools in neighboring states, such as Davidson, Hampden-Sydney, and Washington & Lee, he relied more on his prudence rather than on his enthusiasm. Despite his devout Presbyterianism, he dangled an offer to affiliate the college with other denominations and at one point attempted to persuade Carnegie to guarantee the venture. After the Lexington (Virginia) Presbytery pledged $30,000 to the venture in 1901, it was agreed that the college would affiliate with the Presbyterian Church.

Davis and Elkins then chipped in a modest amount to match the Presbytery. However, when it came to endowing the college, Davis hedged his bet. Even though he had been advised by a representative of the Presbyterian Church that the college should be endowed at a minimum of $2 million, Davis gave $50,000. It was not that he was cheap; he simply displayed caution with the college as he had with Alton Parker. Up to his death in 1916, Davis faithfully covered any deficit incurred by the college. It was a grand gesture that

Above: U.S. President William Howard Taft (third from the left) and Senator Stephen Benton Elkins (fourth from the left) during a visit to Halliehurst, circa 1910.

ensured the college's survival, but not its future.

Although Davis played a larger role, Elkins also was important in the formation of the college. His life was interesting and, for many in West Virginia, mysterious. He arrived in the state via New Mexico, having been a territorial delegate. He met Davis in that capacity in the 1870s. By that time he had already amassed a considerable fortune in railroads and mining. In 1875, he married Davis's daughter Hallie after a whirlwind courtship. Elkins had striking good looks, standing six feet tall and endowed with deep blue eyes, and quickly attracted the equally stunning Hallie. Initially, his entry into West Virginia politics was, at best, somewhat uneasy for Elkins. His activities in the West had him linked in folklore with the outlaw Jesse James. Particularly because his siblings had fought for the South, there were rumors that Elkins also fought for the Confederacy. Of course, these tales proved absurd and, in the end, dissipated. Unlike his father-in-law, Elkins became a Republican.

Not that labels made that big a difference. Henry G. Davis was by no means a partisan, preferring, instead, to stick to the politics of self-interest and parochialism. Helped by his father-in-law, Elkins rose quickly in West Virginia politics; indeed, it has been alleged that Davis helped to "sabotage" an election for the GOP. By the 1880s, Elkins, in the words of one West Virginia politico, "fit in very snugly." As in New Mexico, Elkins became a major businessman in his adopted state. Railroads and mining remained his principal interest, and, like Davis, he became a fierce advocate for a high tariff. Despite the partisan rhetoric that often characterized the era, differences between Davis and Elkins did not amount to much. Davis found his son-in-law to be quite congenial to his interests, and both worked hard to make West Virginia, in essence, a one-party, pro-business state.

However, there was a significant difference between the two. While Davis, aside from the tariff question, satisfied himself politically with West Virginia, Elkins had considerably larger ambitions. A close associate of Senator James G. Blaine, for whom he named one of his sons, Elkins became a significant player in Republican politics. In 1884, Elkins had worked hard to place Blaine in the White House only to see him defeated by Cleveland. When Blaine stepped aside for Benjamin Harrison in 1888, he gained the favor, if not the affection, of the next president of the United States. Blaine became secretary of state in 1889, and, in 1891, he secured for Elkins the position of secretary of war. Davis also had a hand in the appointment, having been a friend of Harrison when the president had served in the Senate. After Cleveland bested Harrison in 1892 in a rematch, Elkins returned to West Virginia. Soon afterwards, Elkins sought and was elected to a Senate seat.

Elkins's relationship with Blaine widened his outlook, particularly in foreign affairs. Like his mentor, he was an ardent imperialist, supporting the annexation of Hawaii in 1893 and later, in 1898, of Cuba and the Philippines. Oddly, he refused to support the entry into war with Spain, but then advocated full exploitation of the spoils. Elkins's reputation as an enthusiastic advocate of expansionism earned him this caption to a cartoon in 1903, claiming that this "ex-territorial attorney general, ex-U.S. district attorney, ex-congressman, and ex-secretary of war—now wants to annex Cuba."

Despite this rather cosmopolitan interest, Elkins remained an "old guard" Republican. Although he applauded Roosevelt's "speak softly and carry a big stick" diplomacy, he still had considerable misgivings about TR's attempts at domestic reforms. He tried, somewhat successfully, to side-track Roosevelt's attempt to regulate railroads in 1906. As a

Opposite: Senator Stephen Benton Elkins

good Republican, he dutifully supported TR for re-election, despite Davis's presence on the opposite ticket. No doubt Davis assured his son-in-law with a gentle wink and a nudge that such a matter caused no strains between them. After all, with Davis, charity always began at home.

It would fall to Davis to rename, for his son-in-law, the town where the college would later be located. Formerly the village of Leadsville, the city of Elkins was the site selected in 1889 for a significant station for the West Virginia and Pittsburgh Railway. The city grew rapidly, thanks to a combination of investments and largesse, courtesy of the two great political powers in the state. Railroads, coal, and timber helped Elkins to expand rapidly and to become the largest city in Randolph County. By 1897, the former village had expanded to ten times the size of its nearest competitor, Beverly. Given that Davis and Elkins paid two-thirds of the taxes in the county, it created considerable alarm when they supported the transfer of the county seat from Beverly to Elkins. After a nasty struggle, Elkins replaced Beverly as not only the economic hub, but the political city of record in Randolph County. Elkins was a creation of the two senators, and it bore the earmarks of both their generosity and their power. In 1901, Davis would establish a bank and, in 1903, a hospital. The next year they founded the college.

Elkins's role in the founding and maintenance of the college was less than Davis's, but that does not mean it should be diminished. His attitude, like his father-in-law's, was quite pragmatic. Indeed, he had looked to the Baptists and Methodists as possible sponsors of the college. It is clear he had a great passion for building "a substantial college" in the town that bore his name. He witnessed the first seven years of the college. He died in 1911 while the college was located on "Sallie Mike Hill" and, like Davis, never witnessed the transfer to Halliehurst Farm in 1926.

But that he and Davis recognized as early as 1891 the importance that a college would have to a community showed great foresight indeed.

Davis and Elkins were by no means unique among industrialists of that period in desiring to place their marks on higher education. In the late nineteenth and early twentieth centuries, industrial magnates gave their names and fortunes to many institutions of higher learning. Indeed, despite the swashbuckling ways many had come by their fortunes, education was viewed with some reverence. In 1904, the year Davis & Elkins was founded, 8,000 communities sponsored Chautauqua events. Thousands flocked to listen to lecturers speak of exotic places and the latest scientific revelations in canopied classrooms. The public was demanding more, believing that if progress was to be the hallmark of the new age, then colleges were the best devices for promoting it.

Rural areas especially, not only in West Virginia but throughout the South, demanded a greater emphasis on education. In the states of North Carolina and Virginia in the early 1900s, higher education, notably of a more practical bent, was promoted and pursued with a religious zeal. It is no accident that Washington & Lee, Hampden-Sydney, and Davidson, two in Virginia and the other in North Carolina, were mentioned as models for D&E. It was also a recognition of what education could do for rural and underdeveloped areas. The insistence on some religious affiliation also spoke volumes about the motivations of the founders. These fortunes were often made with Darwinian social dynamisms, but the industrialists, no doubt Davis and Elkins included, saw the necessity of softening the blow by emphasizing spiritual traditions. Thus in that spirit, Davis & Elkins opened its doors in 1904.

When it opened, Davis & Elkins had a dual function:

Opposite: Hallie Davis Elkins

one as an institution of higher learning, the other as a preparatory school. Neither seemed promising during the first year, seemingly bearing out Davis's caution. Only thirteen students enrolled in the college in September 1904; forty-two enrolled in the preparatory school. By the next year the figures were worse: six students in the college, with fifty pupils in the preparatory school. With its faculty of five, as Thomas Ross stated in 1980 in his *Diamond Jubilee History*, "D&E College must have had the best student-faculty ratio of any college in the nation." Most disheartening, all six were freshmen, leaving the famous five to teach only basic courses. The prep school with its fifty pupils, coupled with the Senator's generosity, kept the college alive. Davis & Elkins was in danger of being a prep school with a college name attached to it. This situation inspired Davis & Elkins's first president, Joseph E. Hodgson, to make an early exit. Despite this dearth of students, the board of trustees, in its infinite wisdom, decided to ban women and become all male. By 1906, the prep school,

thanks largely to the ending of co-education, dropped from fifty to forty-one, inspiring the school paper, *The Acta*, to remark, "How the co-eds are missed! Would they not feel vain did they know the longings of the lonesome." The decision to exclude women, probably through some elitist impulse—the best schools of the day were usually all male —was based largely on ideology rather than any practical consideration. By October 1909, the absurd decision was rescinded.

For administrators of Davis & Elkins, the symbol in the first years probably should have been a revolving door. Three presidents had left in six years, and the college was regarded as little more than a secondary school with a fancy title. James E. Allen became president in 1910 and slowly positioned the college as an institution of higher learning. For twenty-five years he battled, and—it should be said—battled heroically, against immense odds. Bereft of an adequate endowment, forever attempting to prevent the college from departing from its liberal arts mission, and

Student body gathered on campus in the summer of 1923 when the College was located on Sallie Mike Hill

unsuccessfully trying to gain from the board of trustees the funds to upgrade the college, Allen expressed frustrations innumerable. Throughout his tenure faculty salaries were low and, as a result, advanced degrees were few, and the library was forever scorned for its lack of volumes. All of this helped to cost the college accreditation by the North Central Association of Colleges and Schools.

Allen inherited a situation that had improved marginally and only appeared adequate when compared to the desultory standards of the past. In 1911, the second senior class offered up two graduates, the conventional undergraduate population numbered twenty-seven, the prep school students—euphemistically labeled "sub-freshmen"—numbered thirty-nine, and eleven were in a clerical branch. By the fall, the college group soared to thirty-nine, allowing D&E to compete in intercollegiate athletics. For a time, it became difficult for Allen to represent the college as a college rather than a prep school. This situation changed dramatically in the 1920s. In 1919-20, the regular student body numbered 70; by 1926-27, it had risen to 236. With this rise in numbers, Davis & Elkins was able to eliminate the prep school and further its identity as a college. In part, this was due to the rise of football, which was a passion on college campuses. The "boola-boola" spirit of the 1920s helped place the college on the map. D&E, as it so happened, had a superb football program that played a national schedule. "College spirit" was lauded and, in the success-conscious 1920s, education was seen less and less as an option and more of a necessity. High school attendance, a prerequisite for college, grew from 2.2 million in 1919 to five million in 1930. It was not surprising that colleges, with more available to attend, saw a comparable rise. In 1918, only 600,000 were enrolled in colleges; by 1930, 1.2 million attended institutions of higher learning.

Allen, as well, oversaw a vigorous building program that resulted in the 1926 move to the new campus located at the Halliehurst farm. With two academic buildings, the Science

Hall (now known as Albert Hall) and the Liberal Arts Hall, as well as Halliehurst mansion (Graceland was acquired in 1941), the college appeared in far better shape than when Allen arrived. But as with every advance, in the Allen years there were problems—most stemming from the fact that Davis & Elkins seemed hopelessly strapped for cash. The harsh realities of forever operating on a shoestring became vividly apparent when North Central rendered a painful verdict on D&E's request for membership in 1930. Again, the lack of a sufficient library and the endowment difficulties were cited at the top of the list. Salaries were low, few faculty members had advanced degrees, and another problem, not fully appreciated in Elkins, was also identified: the football program.

If Napoleon once quipped that Prussia was hatched from a cannonball, one could assert that D&E's revival had come forth via a football—or that's what the NCA implied. D&E may have had a problem getting a Ph.D. or two, but it had recruited a team that could play with the likes of Army and Virginia. As the report noted, it scheduled no West Virginia teams in the early years. Davis & Elkins had also bent a few rules—it promoted a player who had failed his courses, a practice frowned upon by the NCA.

For Allen, the NCA rejection was a bitter pill to swallow. Given the school's inherent financial problems, he had steadily attempted to improve standards. In 1930, he introduced the concept of a major and a minor and increased the number of credit hours required in the concentration field. Yet Allen left to become president of Marshall College (now University) in June 1935, disappointed by the failure to gain the accreditation that he believed, correctly so, D&E desperately needed. As well, Hallie Elkins's death had robbed him of his "financial angel." For all that, Allen had taken a college in desperate straits and placed it in a position to survive, if not thrive.

In the 1930s, D&E survived and, by its standards, prospered. Its enrollment hovered around 235 in 1935-36, although it declined to 191 in 1939-40. The City of Elkins helped provide some welcome publicity with the introduction of the Mountain State Forest Festival in 1930, an event which is celebrated to this day, primarily on the campus. Through the good offices of a former employee, Jennings Randolph, who was elected to Congress in 1932, President Franklin Roosevelt came to the Forest Festival in 1936. His wife, Eleanor, had given the commencement address at D&E two years before.

Given the bleakness of the economy, Davis & Elkins saw very little growth, but it experienced scarcely any decline. As in earlier days, D&E's programs rose on the strength of its faculty and their students. The theatre department put on some well-regarded plays, and athletics continued to prosper. Yet it was still far removed from the dreams of its founders. Accreditation seemed as far off as ever and the college still lagged behind in necessary facilities, chiefly the library. But, on balance, D&E probably came out ahead, given that many colleges had suffered far worse hits during the 1929-30 stock market crash. In 1939, students looked warily at another war in Europe, unconvinced of America's eventual involvement. Pearl Harbor changed all of that, and on December 7, 1941, the United States was at war with Germany, Italy, and Japan. Like every other American institution, Davis & Elkins was profoundly affected.

At the beginning of the war, Davis & Elkins was still at levels established during the 1930s. In 1942, D&E suspended intercollegiate athletics for the war's duration. The campus was turned into a part-educational and part-military facility. The Civil Aeronautics Administration Training Service Program attracted some 150 cadets. They were billeted in Graceland and fed in Halliehurst. In March 1943, D&E became the headquarters for the 334th Army Air Force College Training Detachment. In 1943-44, 772 aircrew students received training at the college. Training was of such quality that D&E received a grade of "excellent" from the Eastern Training Command. The war proved a boost to the fortunes of the college.

During this period, the college was guided by two vigorous administrators: President Raymond B. Purdum and Dean S. Benton Talbot. They gave leadership comparable to that of James Allen and his paladin, Charles Albert. Purdum doubled the salaries of faculty members and continued the close cooperation with the federal government. Before he became president, Purdum, a professor of chemistry, had already become familiar with federal and military patronage. Even before the war, Purdum attracted the Army and Navy Reserve Programs and the Army Air Corps training unit. He also had a hand in attracting Civil Aeronautics. Despite the war, the college attracted some able faculty members. Though failing to meet the goal of the "Forward-at-Forty" campaign, which was set at $250,000, it came closer than any previous effort. During the campaign, Purdum anticipated, indeed brilliantly so, the opportunities for institutions of higher learning after the war. Noting what came to be known as the G.I. Bill of Rights, or the Serviceman's Readjustment Act of 1944, Purdum, already schooled in the ways of federal aid, positioned the college in a strong way to take advantage of these developments.

That Purdum recognized such an opportunity should not be underestimated or taken for granted. Not all college presidents were as perspicacious or democratic in their views. University of Chicago President Robert Maynard Hutchins sniffed, "Education is not a device for coping with mass unemployment," and further sneered, "Colleges and universities will find themselves converted into educational hobo jungles. And veterans...will find themselves educational hobos." Far from being the case, veterans, as Historian David Kennedy has observed, "were highly motivated students" who gave new life to the institutions of higher learning.

After 1945, veterans streamed into D&E, some still in uniform. They were anticipated and welcomed by faculty already well schooled in how best to meet their special needs. Growth at the college was meteoric, with enrollment increasing from 98 students in 1944-45 to 303 in 1945-46.

President Raymond Purdum at the dedication of Memorial Gymnasium in 1950.

The numbers better than doubled in 1946-47, to 744, of which 447 were veterans. In 1948-49, 941 attended the college, including 878 full-time students. Summer school was also well attended with enrollments as high as 501. Purdum, through his shrewd catering to veterans, had become the academic equivalent of "Crafty Cam" Henderson. But, unlike the football coach, he had cut no corners. Purdum achieved results through planning and by beefing up the faculty and the curriculum.

Purdum's efforts were rewarded by receiving accreditation from the North Central Association—this after years of failure. The NCA noted the improvements in the faculty and the library. Because intercollegiate athletics had been suspended during the war, the old problems with NCA were not a factor. Among the problems remaining, the NCA noticed, was the lack of endowment; "old Henry's ghost" still lingered over the institution. They also rapped the college for expecting its faculty to teach an excessively heavy load. Despite these criticisms, it was clear that Purdum had achieved a major triumph.

But with success came the inevitable problems. As the school grew, it also deviated from its primary liberal arts mission. Courses in nursing, engineering, and elementary education were added to meet the demands of the veteran population. The staggering rise in D&E's student body assumed the form of an academic "bubble." As the 1940s came to an end, the "G.I. generation" became smaller. The school, enjoying its first real taste of success, had also overextended itself.

By 1950, Purdum could still feel confident that Davis & Elkins would enjoy continued progress. In 1951, the Memorial Gymnasium was dedicated. This also closed a chapter in the history of the college, for such a facility

had been hoped for since the 1920s. Yet, the first cracks in the veneer of the post-war student boom were being felt. In 1948-49, enrollment fell to 788, not enough to set off alarm bells, particularly at an institution like D&E, but disturbing just the same. The outbreak of the Korean War in June 1950 dropped enrollment to 625. Purdum, however, never missing a chance to help the military, promoted and established an Air Force Reserve Officer Training Corps at D&E in July 1951. Despite his success, Purdum ended his administration under some criticism for his defense of the religious direction of the college and the traditional liberal arts. This was somewhat ironic because, more than any other D&E president, Purdum had tilted the institution towards the more practical disciplines. As the financial problems increased due to the fall in enrollment, he began to take flack from some citizens of Elkins. He resigned on May 12, 1953, under some pressure. This ended one of the most productive administrations in the history of Davis & Elkins.

Despite its abrupt end, the Purdum administration had made great strides in forming the modern Davis & Elkins College. Besides gaining accreditation, the campus had grown larger in the 1940s, not only in enrollment but physically. Thanks to a gift by the Elkins family of fifty-four acres, the campus grew by 70 percent. Yet, the college faced some daunting problems, partially due to the hangover caused by the "go-go forties." By 1954, the new president, David Allen, had to face the problems of shrinking enrollments and a tight financial situation.

In 1953, the enrollment was 511, of which only 16 were Korean War veterans. The G.I. Bill had contributed much towards D&E success, but the days of big increases in the veterans' population were over. The 1950s also reflected

Opposite (clockwise from upper left): 1959 Cadet Drill Team on front campus;
Dr. Thomas R. Ross presenting Michael Dakes '59 with Air Force ROTC medal in 1958;
Air Cadets at attention at the Elkins Municipal Airport, circa 1940s.

the baby-bust of the 1930s, so traditional students were also in relatively short supply. Hindered, too, by the aggressiveness of state universities in the 1950s, Davis & Elkins had its work cut out for it. The college also struggled with other problems—one in particular—which if uncorrected could have undone much of the progress of the 1940s.

D&E's initial accreditation was up for renewal in 1957, and the college, having been acknowledged as a member of NCA for only ten years, was particularly vulnerable. A team of NCA representatives visited Elkins in January 1957 and were not impressed with what they saw. Questioning D&E's claim of being a liberal arts institution, they charged that it was promoting "extensive offerings in vocational and professional or pre-professional areas." Moreover, they noted that the college offered, outside the traditional bachelor of arts and bachelor of science, four specialized degrees. The entrepreneurial spirit of the G.I. Bill era now became regarded as a strike against D&E. Moreover, faculty salaries and the library had declined to low pre-war standards. They recommended probation and an institutional inspection by NCA of D&E in 1959.

Yet, for all this, there was a bit of hope. North Central's representatives were struck, favorably, by some members of the faculty. Biology, chemistry, and teacher education were singled out for praise. But the history and political science department was especially lauded, not only for its superb academic offerings, but for one individual faculty member. In a not particularly oblique reference, the NCA report praised the head of the department as "an exceedingly able and effective" campus leader. In 1958, this "able and effective" professor was tapped by President Allen to be dean of the faculty.

Thomas Richard Ross assumed the dean's chair in 1958, having served as a history professor since 1949. Having received his doctorate from Harvard, Ross possessed acute academic skills. In the mid-fifties he published a well-

received work on Iowa Senator Jonathan Prentice Dolliver. He also possessed a reputation for integrity and had an immense appetite for hard work. He was and is—and I can attest to it, having served under interim Dean Ross in 1986—an extraordinary politician. Using his considerable skills, he reduced the number of degrees offered at D&E from six to two. Now the B.A. and B.S. were the only degrees conferred. He also enjoyed a collaborative relationship with President Allen. Not since the team of Purdum and Talbot had two officers of the college been in such agreement.

Ross and Allen came closer to building the liberal arts model envisioned by the founders. Although they encouraged the business and economics department, the kudzu-like growth of other professional programs was stopped. In 1959, the NCA revisited Elkins and discovered that the college had not only met its expectations but exceeded them. The probationary period was over, with NCA granting full accreditation to D&E.

Everything they noted had been improved, including salaries and the library. The committee marveled at Dean Ross's heavy workload. Given Allen's fund-raising trips, Ross was "acting president" much of the time, as well as overseeing the library, the admissions office, the registrar, and the dean of students. In between duties, the NCA team noted, he taught two classes as well as supervised independent studies. When queried as to whether he believed he was overworked, Ross answered that he wasn't. It was, to his mind, all in a day's work. The report noted that Ross was "the recognized leader of the faculty" and praised him for taking initiative and creating support for those efforts.

"The current program and its concomitant premises," concluded the NCA report, "are accepted wholeheartedly by faculty, administration, and generally students." Ross took this mandate into the 1960s and placed D&E among some of the most respected institutions in the region. Standards were markedly increased with the introduction of theses and

Opposite: Dr. James E. Allen, Jr., United States Senator Jennings Randolph and President Gordon E. Hermanson at the dedication of Jennings Randolph Hall in 1969.

oral exams at the end of the senior year. During the Allen-Ross partnership, the faculty flourished. William Phipps in Religion, appointed in the fifties, was recognized nationally in 1969 with his book, *Was Jesus Married?* Historians Charles Cullop and James Dow also produced noteworthy efforts. D&E increased the number of its faculty holding doctorates to a consistent level of 40 percent. For this, Ross is to be given the lion's share of the credit. Ross served as dean of the faculty for twelve years, the longest-serving in that office in D&E history.

Credit for the securing of the very vital renewal accreditation goes, as well, to President Allen. He helped restore the financial health of D&E, and contributed to the climate of good feeling on which Dean Ross depended. During Allen's tenure, Science and Liberal Arts Halls were renovated. All areas around the campus were paved. Even the endowment, a persistent headache, improved. Allen announced his retirement in 1964, and was succeeded by Gordon Hermanson.

Hermanson, a graduate of Wheaton College, brought with him a unique background. Involved in missionary work in West Africa and later associate field director of the Presbyterian Synod of Pennsylvania, he brought to D&E the spirit of Christian liberalism. A man of immense energy and physical presence, Hermanson exhibited from the beginning a "can-do" attitude. It was in step with the times —the high point of the New Frontier and its successor the Great Society—when it seemed, in the words of an advisor to President Lyndon B. Johnson, that "the impossible takes a little longer." Hermanson's inaugural address exuded the optimistic nature of the times. "If the college is to achieve new heights," Hermanson proclaimed, "we shall bring it to pass." Consistent with contemporary educational theories, he pointed D&E toward a future of "openness," celebrating "Christian and democratic principles."

For Hermanson, the college he inherited, though in sound financial and academic shape, was too small. When he took over, the enrollment hovered around 600. Indeed, during the first five years of Hermanson's presidency—thanks partially to the first installment of baby boomers—the college grew substantially. In 1964-65, students numbered 597, but by 1969-70, there were 791. By the time of the institutional self-study in 1969-70, D&E was unthreatened by any sanction by NCA. It passed with flying colors.

Yet, something gnawed at Hermanson. Although D&E had done well during his first five years, little had been done to realize, to his satisfaction, that open, democratic, and Christian campus he had so trumpeted in 1964. In his copy of the NCA report, he underlined a number of troubling statements made by the NCA representatives. Three are worthy of notice, in that they reflected Hermanson's angst as to the direction of the college. One lamented the lack of "widespread concern over national, social, and political issues." Another referred to students' desire that "the college would provide and encourage more speakers on controversial subjects." Lastly, they scored the college for "not directly responding to the needs of the Appalachian environment." For Hermanson, changes were essential if he were to achieve his vision.

Those changes came in 1970-71, when Hermanson decided to take a different direction in academic affairs. Dean Ross, who had served Hermanson as loyally and well as he had David Allen, returned to the faculty. With this "dropping of the pilot," came a new academic experiment that would run for nearly ten years. Relying primarily on new faculty members, a great number hired in 1969, Hermanson encouraged integrated studies. In addition, "Woods Orientation" was inaugurated. Admittedly, there was a great feeling of excitement among some faculty and students. Moreover, Dr. Margaret Goddin, daughter of

President Purdum and a dean of the faculty in this period, took the lead in 1973 in founding the Augusta Heritage Center, celebrating the Appalachian region. In 1972, the college contracted with the correctional center at Huttonsville to teach inmates. In the same year, in order to stimulate students, Hermanson commissioned the author of the 1970 NCA Self-Study, Phillips V. Brooks, to attract "controversial" speakers with the IMPACT Program.

It was energy aplenty, with the campus seeing changes nearly every year. Hermanson excelled in bricks and mortar concerns as well. Under his tenure, the Eshleman Science Center, the chapel, and the campus center, which later bore his name, were erected. A number of residence halls were built to house the growing population. By 1978-79, D&E counted some 980 students and would show an increase the next academic year to 1,098. As a reward for all this progress, a new presidential home was built. Hermanson appeared to have realized the vision he had articulated in 1964. Everything bore his stamp; indeed, the letterhead for the college sported a fir tree, a fitting symbol of his commitment to environmentalism and an activist agenda.

Yet, Hermansonian progress and growth came at a price. At the end of his presidency in 1982, the college faced, in the words of the NCA review of 1980, a "serious financial

United States Senator Robert C. Byrd with graduate Robert D. Corregan at commencement 1983.

Halliehurst Mansion, the former home of United States Senator Stephen Benton Elkins and his wife, Hallie Davis Elkins, during its days as a women's residence hall and academic building, circa 1950s.

crisis." Bills were going uncollected and the campus possessed a physical plant that it strained to maintain. Moreover, the academic deanship had fallen into a state of chaos. The office resembled a carousel on which many scrambled to get off; some were equally eager to get on. Faculty interest in the new curriculum would wane, partially because some ardent supporters left the college. The older, more traditional faculty resolutely resisted participating in integrated studies. Times were also changing, bringing the end of integrated multi-disciplined approaches, which were no longer as popular as they had been the decade before.

By 1980, after severe economic problems in the United States, students tired of approaches that were deemed impractical. In the 1970s, integrated studies had been regarded as a way to make the liberal arts "relevant" using dynamic, action-oriented approaches. The 1980 NCA report noted that students had lost their ardor for integrated approaches. Moreover, the liberal arts disciplines of English and history, so involved in integrated studies, saw their own areas decline. The new "relevant" curriculum was the Business Department, led by the resourceful Gloria Marquette Payne, which attracted a disproportionate number of majors.

Hermanson, however, in his eighteen years—the second longest at D&E—had been innovative. For a time, D&E's integrated studies program drew praise from *Time,* the *New York Times,* the *Washington Post,* and the *Christian Science Monitor.* As well, the Augusta Heritage Center was lauded in *US News and World Report.* By the time he left office, Hermanson was beset by demands for a different direction. In 1984, a new president brought a wholly different vision.

Dorothy MacConkey took over at a time when D&E faced

Graceland Mansion, the home of United States Senator Henry Gassaway Davis and his wife, Katherine Bantz Davis, circa 1890s.

problems on a number of fronts. In 1989, the NCA report described the two years after Hermanson, when president replaced president, as a time the college stood "between doldrums and disaster." Perhaps overstated, this nevertheless was an accurate reflection of the attitudes of townspeople and, of course, the NCA team view. Also, professors who had chafed under Hermanson's reforms eagerly applauded MacConkey's first efforts at changing course. By 1987, integrated studies was a memory, replaced by a traditional liberal arts core. Even the "winter term," a Hermanson innovation, was repealed. Faculty salaries, especially at the senior end, saw significant raises in the first five years of MacConkey's presidency. But her greatest successes were with the community, the board of trustees, and the NCA, in which she would play an important role.

"Town and gown" relations had deteriorated during the Hermanson years, particularly regarding two dilapidated

mansions on the campus, Halliehurst and Graceland. Both, by 1985, resembled haunted houses. Hermanson, whose architectural taste ran to the modern, had never been particularly enthusiastic about maintaining or restoring these buildings. A number of prominent Elkins citizens, spearheaded by Ralph and Mary Frances Shepler, formed a committee to "save" Halliehurst. In 1984, impatient with what they felt was wanton neglect of two historical treasures, this committee questioned if D&E was, in fact, going to survive to oversee improvements. This was the perception that, by 1985, was pervasive in the Elkins community. MacConkey embraced this cause without hesitation, offering to "save" Halliehurst, a sentiment echoed by the local paper. By the end of her term, she had restored Halliehurst (1990), having it declared a national historic landmark in 1988, and Graceland (1996). These mansions, together with Liberal Arts and Albert Halls, the Ice House, Boiler House, and

The Presidents of Davis & Elkins College

Joseph E. Hodgson
1904-1905

Frederick H. Barron
1905-1906

Marshall C. Allaben
1906-1910

Robert T. Liston
1940-1943

Raymond B. Purdum
1944-1954

David K. Allen
1954-1964

James E. Allen
1910-1935

Charles E. Albert
1936-1939

Harry E. Whetsell
1940
Acting President

Gordon E. Hermanson
1964-1982

C. Brent DeVore
1982-1984

Dorothy I. MacConkey
1985-1998

President G. Thomas Mann
1998-

Gatehouse, were declared a National Historic district.

MacConkey restructured the board of trustees by replacing clergy with predominately business leaders. In the early years she was a prodigious fund-raiser, and this was partially due to her success with the board. In this task MacConkey excelled, with an energetic style and a colorful personality. She formed the modern board at D&E, answering a concern of NCA in its 1980 report, and made a commitment to a new library which she saw to completion in 1992.

MacConkey received a glowing tribute from the NCA in 1989. She was listed as the number one asset, having "restored faith in the future of Davis & Elkins." Unlike 1980, there were no progress reports required and no conditions imposed. It was an impressive start, with great accomplishments in the past and some waiting in the future. Yet, the president so hailed in 1989 that one local banker gushed, "This is the best president ever," would have some choppy moments in the 1990s.

As the mansions were renovated and the library constructed, faculty salaries, after 1988, began to stagnate. For the years 1989-1992, the faculty did not receive substantial raises. As the president's office, formerly housed in Liberal Arts Hall, moved to Halliehurst, a psychic distance between MacConkey and the faculty grew. In a divisive decision, MacConkey dismissed a popular dean of the faculty and replaced him with one who had less support. Faculty-administration relations began to deteriorate rapidly. Enrollments, strong until 1995, began to decline. By 1997, fiscal problems began to emerge. In 1997, she announced her retirement. As with Purdum and Hermanson, MacConkey had overseen tremendous growth and, at her height, had been enormously successful. Yet, like her predecessor, she left the college with shrinking enrollments and increasing debts. MacConkey had achieved much; however, most of the progress of those years concerned construction.

It was under these clouds that G. Thomas Mann assumed

the presidency on July 1, 1998. He quickly acted to ameliorate the budget crisis, cutting some positions, and tried to reduce D&E's "smorgasbord" curriculum. However, it was a rocky first two years, with budget surprises semiannual. At one occasion, President Mann referred to them as "hiccups," with the tone of a man who was not trying to be funny. However, the unsnarling and unraveling process began to pay off. By 2001, the budget was becoming manageable and enrollments began to stabilize and, by 2002, even increase.

More good news arrived in September 2002 when *US News and World Report*, in its annual assessment of colleges, placed Davis & Elkins among the top comprehensive liberal arts colleges in the South. Some inkling of this progress was evident in the NCA review of March 2000. Reviewers were highly impressed with the faculty and pleased with the dedication shown by the D&E community during the crisis. Despite problems, D&E received a generally favorable review, with progress reports expected in enrollment and finance. The other expectation was in curriculum assessment, which had been essentially unaddressed in the 1990s. In 2003, D&E cleared all these hurdles, receiving praise from the NCA.

Mann made progress in other areas, as well. As David Allen had forty years before, he appointed a popular faculty member as dean of the faculty. Also like Allen, Mann recommitted Davis & Elkins to its liberal arts core, dutifully factoring in changes that had occurred over the years.

Despite its challenges, Davis & Elkins has persisted and prospered. Throughout its first century, one constant has been the chemistry between faculty, staff, and the student body. Often enough, NCA cited the dedication of the faculty to their mission. In report after report, this was a uniting factor over the decades. And, of course, the students' enthusiasm, has always made attending the college a rich experience. On the playing fields, in the classrooms, or even under the trees, regardless of circumstance, D&E enriched even when it had to endure.

Athletics at Davis & Elkins College

June 27, 1935, must have been a difficult day for Eli Camden "Cam" Henderson. Having compiled a marvelous record at Davis & Elkins College in the twenties and a good part of the thirties, he now awaited a decision by the board of trustees. Henderson received what amounted to a vote of no confidence by the board for overspending and committing infractions in regard to player eligibility. This ended a great era of gridiron success for Davis & Elkins.

But it also said a lot about the college's commitment to academic excellence and to fairness. Despite the fact that Henderson enjoyed great support in the town and a legendary reputation in the state, the board of trustees dismissed him for financial and other transgressions. North Central had already chastised the college for placing football way too high on its list of priorities. Indeed, as we have seen, it cost D&E accreditation in 1930.

Opposite: Cam Henderson

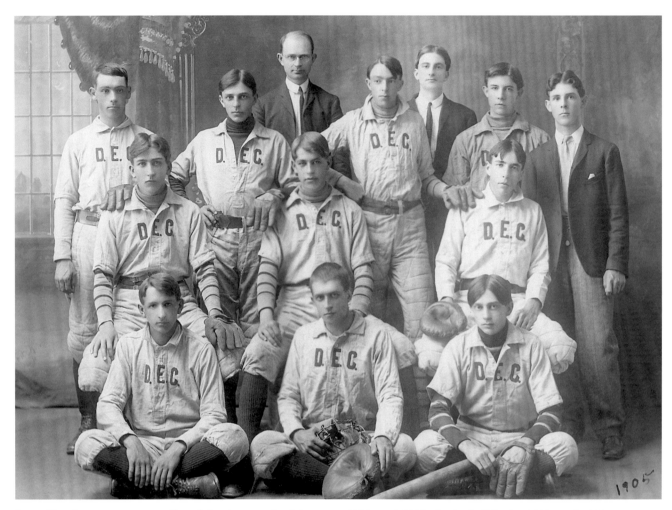

Some Henderson supporters alleged that it seemed mighty strange that the termination of "Cam" came after his first losing season in memory in 1934. However, the consensus is that the faculty and trustees simply had had enough of, as Thomas Ross states, "the athletic tail wagging the academic dog." Henderson then went to Marshall College where he compiled an outstanding record.

Perhaps Davis & Elkins was, in the words of Henderson biographer Sam Clagg, "too small a pond to have a boulder hurled into it the size of Cam Henderson." Indeed, Clagg has a point: Henderson was not just a good coach, he was an outstanding one. Despite limited D&E resources, he coached highly competitive teams and, in the halcyon days of the twenties, mauled many an opponent. And all of this was done in some cases without assistant coaches. But in 1935, D&E made a decision that was painful, yet, in its view, necessary. Having to choose between an aspiring scholastic program or a proven athletic one, it chose academics. D&E's history includes many highlights in athletics: football in the

1920s and 1930s, basketball in the 1940s and 1950s, soccer in the late 1960s and 1970s, and women's field hockey in the 1960s and 1970s; add to that consistent programs in track and baseball. Yet when athletic push met academic shove, academics proved the victor.

The student-athlete, as hackneyed as it sounds, remained a priority at D&E. Perhaps the institution was driven strictly by budget constraints, but even more so by conviction. Vince Lombardi's dictum that "winning's not everything, it's the only thing" never held sway at Davis & Elkins. It was a tempting apple and, at times, difficult not to pick, but athletic glory at a prohibitive price was eschewed by D&E. Nevertheless, it must have been exceedingly difficult to relieve Henderson, who was a diadem in Davis & Elkins's crown. For the gray thirties, it took a great deal of principle to release such an outstanding football legend.

The football teams that Davis & Elkins fielded in the Henderson era were legendary. At their height, they played the likes of Army and Virginia and dominated what ever

unfortunate team they could hustle onto the schedule in the neighboring area. As befitting the 1920s, D&E's exploits were celebrated in the press—even in the *New York Times*. A D&E banner floated over Harry's American Bar in Paris —with the likes of Harvard and Yale. If Fordham had its "Seven Blocks of Granite" and Notre Dame its "Four Horsemen of the Apocalypse," D&E was known by the moniker "the Scarlet Hurricane."

And blow it did throughout West Virginia. Henderson, who arrived from Muskingum College in 1923, compiled an undefeated season during his first year at the college. Rio Grande was the first victim at 56-0; then a squeaker against Western Maryland 14-6, a blowout versus Morris Harvey 54-0, a squeaker against Broaddus College 13-7, a rout over

Fairmont State College 52-0, and, finally, a clinching of "the Class B" championship over Salem College 47-3. The schedule improved; though the dominance lessened, it wasn't by much. In 1925, D&E barely lost to West Virginia University and Army. Otherwise, they overwhelmed the rest 244 points to 32. The most impressive loss was to Army just a week after the Black Knights had mauled Notre Dame— Army won a squeaker 14-6.

Davis & Elkins's efforts brought this tribute in the sports section of the *New York Times*: "The visitors brought a well-coached team which had a smooth working attack," the newspaper explained, adding that D&E was "equipped with plenty of baffling formations." It also praised Henderson's squad for tackling "hard but cleanly." The crowd at Michie

---

Above: 1948 Cheerleaders (left to right) Louise Hanson, Denny Mays, Emma Mae Stalnaker, John Moser, Lemoyne Hamilton, Richard Mays
Opposite: The 1905 Davis & Elkins College baseball team posed for its team photograph in a downtown Elkins studio. Members include: (front row, left to right) Maxwell, Irons, Knote; (second row) Grove, C. Rease, unknown; (third row) Hutson, unknown, Ward, Harper, Marsteller; (fourth row); Davis & Elkins College President J.E. Hodgson and team manager Wilverton

Stadium was greatly impressed—they would not be the last. In the following seasons, victories over regional and national powers would come. D&E beat WVU two years in a row, 1928 and 1929. It also upset the midshipmen of Navy 2-0 in 1928. Its players came from all over the country—Albert Hawley from Montana, Elijah Smith from Wisconsin, and Alva "Chief" Wagner from Minnesota, to name a few.

Not only did Henderson shine, he was aided by a crack director of intercollegiate athletics and publicity. Jennings Randolph, an instructor in public speaking, brought to his position a flair that bordered on brilliance. He would serve from 1926 to 1932, leaving only after winning a congressional seat. In 1958, he was elected to the United States Senate, where he served until 1985. Randolph coined the nickname "Crafty Cam" and played up the exploits of both the football and basketball teams. Each served the interest of Cam Henderson who coached the two sports. Randolph was a "boulder" of publicity, outmatching his competitors. Even in later years, in a documentary by Ken Burns on Huey Long, Randolph described the appeal of Louisiana's kingfish in thrilling detail. If Henderson was served as well by Randolph as Randolph managed to serve Huey Long in a mere documentary, he received exceptional service. Randolph created a legend on the D&E campus and became a legend by serving West Virginia with distinction in the U.S. Senate.

Football, however, waned in popularity at D&E. The years passed and the glory of the 1920s and '30s faded. On NCA recommendations, the schedule was trimmed to local and regional teams, the money ran out, and the buccaneer recruiting style of Henderson was eliminated. In 1961, after one desultory season after the other, D&E terminated football. Although Henderson's gridiron glory had come at a price, it still remains the most exciting era in D&E athletic history. However, D&E was not the only school that suffered a comedown from twenties' glory; many a power—

Fordham and Columbia come to mind—also experienced similar declines.

Basketball flourished as well under Henderson. His 1924 team went undefeated—beating both Catholic University and George Washington University. After those defeats of Washington, D.C. squads, Shirley Povich gave the "men from the hills" the "Scarlet Hurricane" name that ultimately stuck to the football team. Randall "Rand" McKinney played from 1925-28 on squads that accrued 105 wins to only 8 losses. WVU, in one season, was dealt the hat trick by D&E, losing three times. McKinney went on to be inducted into the West Virginia Sportswriters Association Hall of Fame.

Unlike football, basketball did not suffer the same kind of decline after Henderson left. His successors were highly competent, led by Harry L. "Bud" Shelton. Although Shelton was a good football coach, he was exceptional in basketball. He recruited Peter "Press" Maravich, who was elected president of the student body in 1939. In later years, Press would coach at D&E, go on to serve West Virginia Wesleyan College, then North Carolina State in the same capacity, and finish his career at Louisiana State University. While in Baton Rouge, he introduced the world to his greatest legacy, his son Peter "Pistol Pete" Maravich. During his career in the late sixties, the younger Maravich would bedazzle audiences with unbelievable ball handling and scoring ability. He gained recognition in the National Basketball Association and later was enshrined in the Basketball Hall of Fame. Another associated with D&E hoops who went on to fashion an outstanding coaching career at Marshall and at Wake Forest University was Carl Tacy (class of 1956).

In the late 1940s, Robert N. "Red" Brown assembled one of the finest of D&E's basketball teams. Ably assisted by Maravich, Davis & Elkins went 16-8 in 1947-48, ranking third in the conference. They went on to win the tournament by spanking West Virginia Wesleyan 81-54. The team had an outstanding threesome: James "Hap" Huey at center, Joe

Ceravola at guard, and the legendary Carl Payne at forward. Some have called it "the greatest team ever to wear the maroon and white of Davis & Elkins." The last statement begs a question: What are the colors of D&E—"Scarlet Hurricane," or "maroon and white," or the present bright red and white? Whatever shade D&E basketballers wore, in the 1940s the uniform was a source of great pride to the school.

Payne, a native of Elkins, was and is particularly remembered for his electrifying play. Along with his team-mate Huey, he was named three times to the all-tournament and all-conference teams. His teams won the conference championship in 1949-50 and went to the National Intercollegiate Basketball Tournament in Kansas City, Missouri, losing to the University of Tampa in the semi-finals. The "Fabulous Five" were led in scoring by Huey with 2,104 points, a D&E record. Other members of that legendary "five" were Carl Payne, Joe Ceravolo, Ted Chizmar, and Joe Pukach. Payne was known as "Mr. Basketball" and is generally regarded as the best all-around cager in D&E history.

Payne represents in many regards the spirit of the 1940s. Like many of his fellow students, he had served in the United States Army during World War II. Fighting in the European

Above: Football coaches Press Maravich and Ace Federovitch, 1950

Theatre of Operations, Payne earned a Bronze Star, the third-highest decoration in the armed services. His legacy to his alma mater and to the community of Elkins, which he served so well, lasted until his death at age 69 in 1993. In 1950, he married Gloria Marquette who later distinguished herself as the legendary long-term chair of the business and economics department.

After the "Fabulous Five," the program did well for a short time. Under Maravich it went 15-7 in 1950-51. When Maravich left the program, it continued to be reasonably successful. "Bud" Shelton returned, aided by a large—at that time—six foot, five inch center, Paul Wilcox. He scored 46 points over West Virginia Wesleyan on January 12, 1954. However, academics tripped up Mr. Wilcox and another outstanding player, causing D&E to end up with a mediocre 14-13 record. Yet, the next season, having mended their scholastic ways, the two players, Wilcox and Miles Runner, returned, leading the team to a 17-7 record and placing second in the conference. After those years, D&E's basketball

program began to founder and winning seasons came less frequently. An exception was in 1958-59, when Wilcox and Runner returned from military service and D&E registered 16 wins against 12 losses. After that, the decline progressed vigorously.

Although men's basketball suffered a decline, women cagers enjoyed considerable success. In 1954-55, the women's varsity team enjoyed a decent season, ably coached by Louise Linhart. Nancy McFarlane, in the 1970s, produced some outstanding squads. In 1977, McFarlane's Senators won first place in the West Virginia Intercollegiate Athletic Association (WVIAA). Led by Pam Boyd, who scored 39 points in a game, it was an outstanding team. McFarlane continued to produce respectable teams into the 1980s. Players from the McFarlane era who garnered high honors were Karen Crump, Cheryl Novoshielski, and Cindy Stinger.

Another women's sport that shone at D&E was field hockey. Its first season commenced in 1949, coached by an instructor in physical education, Betsy Crothers. In the

Above: 1981-1982 Women's Basketball players #14 Nancy Davis and #42 Peggy Hughes
Opposite: 1949-50 men's conference championship team that went on to the National Intercollegiate Basketball Tournament
in Kansas City, losing to University of Tampa in the semi-finals

1960s and 1970s, it was ably coached by Jean Minnick (then Tallman). A brilliant tactician and taskmaster, she molded some outstanding teams. In 1964-65, Minnick's squads posted an undefeated record. Her teams also competed in Division I of the NAIA. In 1975 and 1976, D&E won the championship in West Virginia and went undefeated in 1977 and 1978. They distinguished themselves in the Region 5 tournament, defeating Indiana and Michigan State, and went on to compete for the national championship in Ellensburg, Washington. Such players as Christine Smith, Cindy Paulmier, and Tess Werner performed brilliantly on the field. Coach Minnick, who was also recognized as a superb professor, developed a first-class program.

However, this field hockey version of the Scarlet Hurricane

*Above: Coach Nancy Schaub, Coach Jean Minnick, Cindy Stinger and Coach Nancy McFarlane when Stinger
(a three sport athlete – field hockey, basketball and softball) was honored in 1981 as Davis & Elkins College Athlete of the Year.*

would fizzle out. As Title Nine allowed women to compete in more sports, the talent increasingly went towards soccer and basketball. By the 1990s, D&E had a national schedule which sent its teams as far as Palo Alto to find schools that still played the sport. It became expensive and, as with football, undefeated seasons were transformed into no-win campaigns. In the late 1990s, D&E ended its once memorable association with field hockey.

Despite its fate, field hockey and Jean Minnick left a glorious legacy for D&E. The enthusiasm, in good and bad seasons, typified Davis & Elkins athletics. Certainly, Minnick must be ranked among D&E's great coaches. Her field hockey teams set a standard that her successors could not sustain. It must be said, however, that these later teams

Above left: 1988 Field Hockey Players #10 Nancy Peterson and #1 Michele Michalick
Above right: 2000 Soccer Players #13 Amanda Loveland, #16 Gabriella Hutchison and #15 Nora Miller

the upstart nature of soccer in the United States in the early sixties, Davis & Elkins scheduled some non-varsity games, one of which was against a team "from" WVU, winning by a tally of 5-0. The season ended at 3-5, but D&E won every home game and indeed, did not allow a goal. It was an auspicious start.

Beginning in 1968, the footballers, in the international sense of the term, began an era that would have impressed Cam Henderson. Coach Gregory Myers and his booters went undefeated in the regular season and swept the NAIA's District Six championship. They moved on to the national championship, defeating Quincy College. Led by Rildo Ferreira and William "Scotty" Smyth, they transformed Davis & Elkins into an NAIA soccer power. In 1970, Myers' team once again gained soccer supremacy in the NAIA, defeating Quincy 2-0. Mike Udofia, Bill Nuttall, and Nils Heinke joined Smyth on the all-tournament team. Nuttall also gained further laurels, being named Most Valuable Player in the tournament. It would be Myers' last appearance as D&E's soccer coach; he left to pursue a doctorate and to coach at the Naval Academy. Charles Smith then took over the helm and the winning continued. Once again, D&E made it to the final game; however, it lost in a rematch with Quincy 1-0. It was the last match for "Scotty" Smyth, closing out a remarkable career. He was named MVP in the NAIA finals in 1968 and 1969. In 1971, he was all-tournament, along with Heinke and Ekong Etuknwa.

Fred Schmalz succeeded Smith and D&E continued to win. In 1972, they lost narrowly in the national championship to Westmont College, 2-1. They would make a final appearance in 1974, losing to rival Quincy 6-0. Despite not winning a championship, Schmalz's teams were contenders in every year he was coach, save 1975. Schmalz continued the

were handicapped by a national trend away from the sport and, in the end, were forced to schedule opponents with far greater resources.

National attention for another sport garnered recognition for Davis & Elkins. Soccer, in the late 1960s thru the 1970s and for a considerable time in the 1980s, proved D&E's most enduring winner. The soccer program replaced football in 1961 as the premier fall sport at the college. The first soccer match was played on October 18, 1961, as D&E hosted rival West Virginia Wesleyan. D&E won by a score of 2-0. Given

Above: Cheerleader Maryellen Mahon looks on as Greg Myers, men's soccer coach, 1968-1971, paces the sidelines during a 1969 game.

There's no shortage of excitement when the D&E Men's Soccer Team takes the field!
Overleaf: 1970 men's N.A.I.A. National Championship soccer team

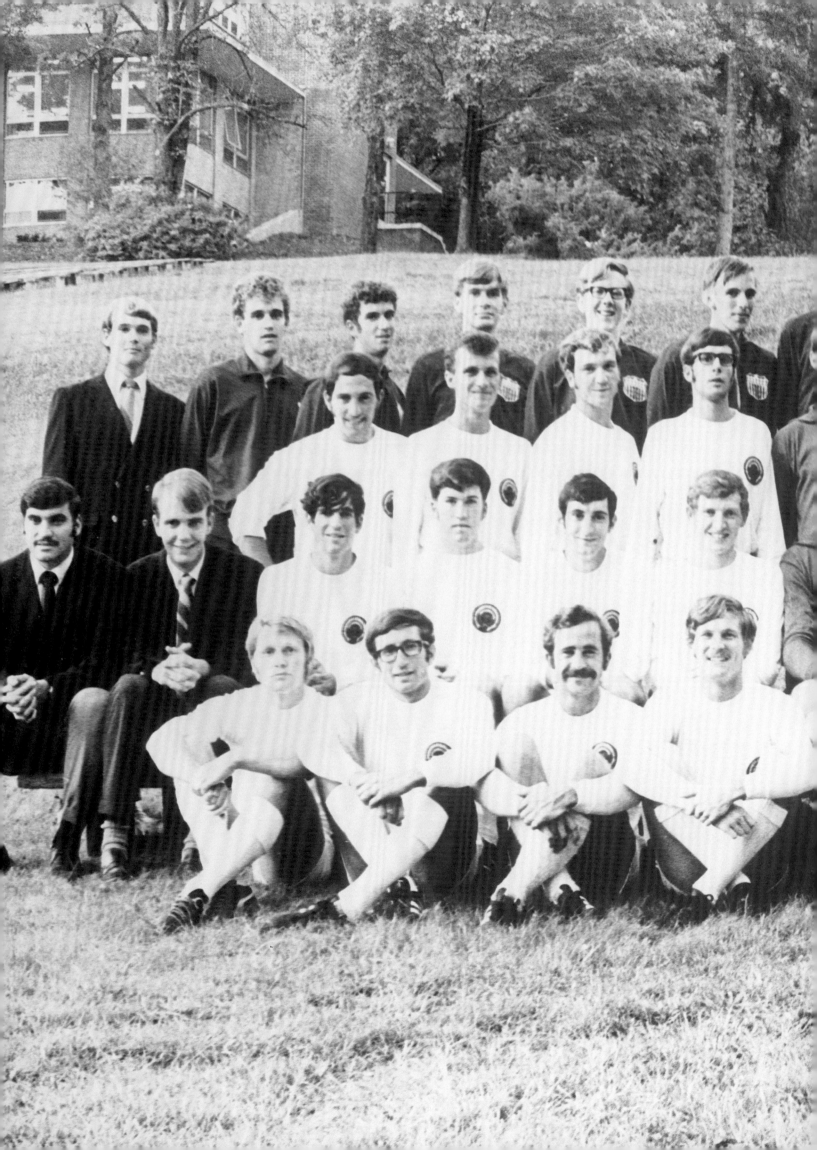

tradition set by Myers. He won many awards and his leaving D&E in 1979 was acutely felt. He was succeeded by Nils Heinke, who continued to be competitive into the 1980s.

In D&E's championship years, the Hurricane resembled more a tornado as the soccer juggernaut twisted swiftly downfield, making sharp quick cuts at the goal. Defensively, it also demonstrated considerable prowess. In 1973, Conn Davis proved that he was a world-class goalie, setting a record 22 saves against Howard University. They needed every one of them, for D&E won by only 1-0. The performance of the booters was noticed in the admittedly small world of professional soccer in the 1970s. Smyth and Nuttall were selected to play professionally, and Hank Steinbrecher became a leader in the business end of the U.S. Soccer Federation.

Soccer was respectable, even competitive, in the 1980s, but it never regained the glory of the 1970s. Alderson-Broaddus and West Virginia Wesleyan began to challenge D&E's dominance. Alderson-Broaddus appeared in the finals in 1981 and was trounced by D&E's old nemesis, Quincy, 4-1. Wesleyan, beginning in 1984, won the first of five championships. As competition became more acute, D&E declined from national power, to regional contender, to back of the pack. Money once more intruded, with international scholarships earmarked for the sport eliminated. As a member of the NCAA Division II, D&E has been not even a blip on the board.

Which is a shame, for soccer had—and has—added to Davis & Elkins in a fashion unrelated to sports. Its international players added a perspective in the classroom that is not easy to find. With Venezuelans, Trinidadians, Chileans, Irishmen, and others, D&E soccer helped to truly internationalize the campus. Once more, cost accounting brought an end to the dominance of a sport that brought

considerable recognition to the school and which was a source of great pride.

Yet, despite the descent from glory, Davis & Elkins athletes have displayed determination on the field of play. Operating under disadvantages galore, those who commit themselves to hours of practice and play have earned the admiration of the Davis & Elkins community. And, in some areas, the high standards of the past have been maintained. Baseball, dating from 1905, in recent years produced some good teams. In the year 2000, they carved out a 27-19 season. The golf team, which featured the Dortmund brothers, Paul and Lee, led D&E into NCAA post-season competitions. The women's basketball team has had some good runs and has received national recognition for the academic achievement of its team members.

Perhaps a symbol of D&E commitment to clean competition can be best illustrated by the cross-country teams. Led by Will Shaw, who also deserves a salute for managing athletics during lean times, the runners have demonstrated success in hard years. The runners, around three o'clock in the afternoon, have become ubiquitous in downtown Elkins. Their spirit, selflessness, and devotion to their sport is based entirely on love of the activity. The present director of intercollegiate athletics, Ralph Hill, can take comfort in knowing that, despite adversity, there is considerable pride.

Under a new director, D&E continues on into the 21st century with a desire that its athletic past will be a harbinger for its future. Hopeful that new facilities will replace old ones and confident that financial fortune will once more smile on the institution, Davis & Elkins athletics continues on its journey with the same determination and good cheer as its three o'clock cross-country runners.

Clockwise from above left: Original Halliehurst Farm swimming pool;
John "Ace" Federovitch holding up his end of the bargain . . . Basil Sharp in the late 1930s;
Lance Pledger '69 (left) leading the pack; Austin Wilder goes in for an easy lay-up during the 1982-1983 campaign.

Davis & Elkins College Gallery

*Over the years: a collective look at the campus,
the people and the activities of Davis & Elkins.*

*Members of Fi Batar Cappar, faux fraternity in front of Science Hall (now Albert Hall), circa 1928. During the 1924 football season,
a pep fraternity known as the Iota Phi Theta appeared on the Davis & Elkins campus. On the occasion of the Davis & Elkins – West Virginia
University football game at Morgantown, October 3, 1925, Iota Phi Theta was made a chapter of Fi Batar Cappar,
a well-known mock fraternity, having chapters in many schools in the East and on the West coast.
Opposite: Henry Gassaway Davis, "He worked as if he would live forever. He lived as if he would die to-morrow."*

Top: Campus panorama (left to right): Albert Hall, Liberal Arts Hall, Jennings Randolph Hall and Booth Library;
Below: Science Center gazebo in winter; A lazy summer day on the Halliehurst lawn; Front campus
Opposite (top): William S. Robbins Centennial Tower of the Madden Student Center, dedicated March 19, 2004.
Below (left to right): Game Room; Tower interior; Cadillac Daddy Café seating area

Top left: Grady F. Guye '49 and Ralph Hess present Mary Frances Shepler with contributions to the restoration of Halliehurst mansion in 1992. Top right: Eshleman Science Center; Center: Gary North '62 escorts Mountain State Forest Festival Queen Silvia XXV, Rebecca Bess, on the occasion of her Royal Coronation in October, 1961. The Trainbearers were William Nietzold and David Williams; the Crownbearer was Jonathan Keith Hiser, son of Davis & Elkins College physics professor J. Keith Hiser. Below right: Harry "Bud" Shelton '34 and wife Kathryn Shelton '36 join Gloria Marquette Payne '43 and husband Carl Payne '50 to show their D&E pride.

Robbins Chapel at night with Hermanson Campus Center in background

Above: Liberal Arts Hall trimmed with a dusting of snow
Below: Albert Hall in springtime.

Above: Women's Residence Hall – Halliehurst portico room, circa 1940s.
Below: Modern Women's Residence Hall – my how things have changed!
Overleaf: (left page) Post-Restoration Graceland Mansion, home of the Graceland Inn and Conference Center, Erickson Alumni Center
and Robert C. Byrd Center for Hospitality and Tourism (right page) Post-Restoration Halliehurst Mansion (large photograph),
current home of the College's administrative offices; Pre-Restoration Halliehurst Mansion (small photographs)

Clockwise from top left: Stairway to Presidential Hall;
Woods Orientation 2002; A crisp fall day
studying on the Halliehurst lawn; Catchin' some rays

Clockwise from top left: Associate Professor of Physics Brian Moudry with students Gabbe Hutchison '03 and Lisa Hartman;
Associate Professor of English William King with students Nina Bajaj and Stephanie Perry '03;
NASA astronaut Heidi Piper, right, presents ROTC cadet Carmel Shearer '82 with her Silver Snoopy Award;
Associate Professor of Economics Nadeem Khan with students Tiffany Holmes, Hill Lappen '01 and Yoshie Shirao '01

[1]

[2]

DAVIS AND ELKINS vs. SALEM COLLEGE

[3]

ADELPHI
vs.
DAVIS-ELKINS

[4]

[5]

John Whitman

[6]

[7]

[8]

[1] 1932-33 D&E basketball team: (front row, left to right): Coach Jennings Randolph, Whitey
Kendall, Bill Tinney, Coach Cam Henderson (back row, left to right)
Fred Heavner, Thurman Hodges, Ellis Vest, Harry Shelton, Clay Martin;
[2] 1911 D&E baseball team [3] 1938 D&E football program;
[4] 1955 D&E basketball program; [5] D&E cross country runner Christopher Keish '90;
[6] Members of an early 1940s Davis & Elkins football team; [7] A lady Senator returns serve;
[8] The 1975-76 Davis & Elkins Cheerleading Squad: (bottom): Karen Gallagher; (top center):
Jane Saylor, Dierdre Jordan, Gail Soliwoda, Denise Harrell and Cecelia Long

Clockwise from top left: (left to right) 1996 Mountain State Forest Festival Maid of Honor Meg Dailer, Queen Silvia LX Alison Jo Hood '97, and Maid of Honor Lori Casey pose before the marble fireplace in Halliehurst after the Royal Coronation; April Deitsch '04 and Alexis Kincaid '04 enjoy a back-to-school ice cream social; The West Virginia Highlanders of Davis & Elkins College, circa 1990; Stairway to Gribble Hall

*Top: Biology Department Chair Michelle Mabry in the Eshleman Science Center greenhouse
with students Erin Gamrod '01 and Jamie Hicks '02; Below: Shhhh! It's study time in the Booth Library*

*Clockwise from upper left: Woods Orientation; Dr. Gloria Marquette Payne '43 and Stephanie St. Hilaire at commencement 2000;
commencement 2004; posing in and on the caboose at the soccer field in the 1990s; 1946 May Queen Beth Guye (Kittle) and escort Jim McGee.*

Top: Gatehouse; Below left: Cathleen Huet '87 and Jon Morrison '88 perform in Night of the Iguana *in the Boiler House Theater in 1986.*
Below right: Music in the afternoon on the pre-restoration Halliehurst front porch, circa 1982.

Service First: Faculty and Staff

You would think that summer was a time to relax, a period to take stock of the last academic year and give yourself a well-deserved rest. This may be considered proper for most, but some show exceptional dedication to their work and labor without giving a thought to their own comfort. Dr. Gloria Marquette Payne, longtime chairperson of the Business and Economics department, is one who regards summer as just another time to display her dedication to service.

During one "B" term of summer school, I witnessed Dr. Payne tutoring one student for the full two hours of the class in which he was the sole participant. She cannot be accused of being mercenary—that one student certainly did not benefit her financially, since summer school pay is based on enrollment. Yet, the student needed the course and Payne showed no hesitation in giving him what amounted to a personal audience. Some may have assigned readings and been done with it—but not Payne.

Opposite: S. Benton Talbot, a long-time dean and professor of biology, in his office.

She regards meeting students' needs as central to her mission and therefore cheerfully offered her services—to the immense benefit of the student. Payne has been associated with D&E since 1939 when she arrived as a student. She excelled both in and beyond the classroom. For example, she was named Queen of the May Fete in 1942, a significant barometer of popularity in those days. Later she wed basketball star Carl Payne. She returned to the College in 1945 as a member of the faculty, later earning the Ph.D. at the University of Pittsburgh. All this was done while working a full-time job and rearing a family. Due to her fierce dedication to students and her academic discipline, Payne has built a loyal following among students and alumni. She even holds a faculty chair specifically given in her name—a high honor indeed. Recipient of the Lois Latham Award for teaching excellence as well as numerous state, regional, and national awards, she personifies a spirit of personalized education and personal regard for those in her charge.

Payne is not alone: many exceptionally dedicated faculty members have left indelible marks on D&E through the years. In biology, there is a long tradition extending from S. Benton Talbot to James Van Gundy; in political science,

Dr. Gloria Marquette Payne '43 Business and Economics professor lecturing in class

from Dorothy Roberts to Thomas Chadwick. These are to
name but a few of the truly outstanding professors in D&E's
history. Not all the professors were alike; many used different
methods and adhered to various pedagogical styles, but
many were unusually effective in equipping graduates with
the skills required to survive in the marketplace and excel in
their professions.

In support of the faculty have been countless staff
members preparing the groundwork for success. Over the
often-troubled history of D&E, they have provided stability
and brought an ample dose of good humor to their work.
Secretaries have been called upon to help prepare reports
and work closely with administrators on immensely important projects. Faculty members have been called out of the

Dr. Thomas Richard Ross

classroom to perform critical service alongside their
colleagues in administration. One faculty member, describing
this cooperative spirit, remembers that D&E "had little
in material things in 1944, but it had a strong Christian
faculty, with optimism, vision, and courage." Ironically,
Dr. Georgianne Stary, an education and psychology
professor from 1944 to 1954, had initially been a pessimist,
believing that all talks of growth were "a bit pathetic and
unrealistic" but confessed that the longer she stayed, the
more she "caught the spirit."

Under President Purdum, the "spirit" was channeled into
obtaining regional accreditation in 1946. Stary, who by then
had gone from pessimism to passionate optimism, fondly
remembered how "Mrs. Purdum got up at two in the

Dr. Georgianne Stary

S. Benton Talbot Biology Seminar

morning to make us coffee and Brunswick stew to keep us awake and fortified until the job might be finished and sent out on the next plane." She described a community selfless in its desire to improve the place and to succeed. Solving problems "lay in the careful planning by the administration and faculty working together," she concluded.

This has been a secret behind D&E's successes—selfless respect and regard for the larger community. In this respect, John Stuart Mill or William James may have looked favorably on this small college in North Central West Virginia. Countless accreditation reports have cited this spirit and, in some cases, zeal for its success. Because of it, D&E has often chosen to change its identity while keeping this "spirit" of altruism for students and community alive. It has also contributed to a unique atmosphere and a quite different definition of who administrators, staffers, and faculty members are and what they do.

Throughout its history, utility has been a watchword at D&E. Dr. Thomas Richard Ross frequently taught history courses while serving as dean—a practice continued under Laurence McArthur in biology. Presidents, as well, have also graced the classroom—a practice, when time permits, continued by Thomas Mann. Wherever someone's talent is needed, it is used. Hunter Davis, an English professor, played a key role in formation of the soccer teams of the 1960s. In the 1970s, nearly all professors pitched in with the promotion of the interdisciplinary core curriculum of that period. As with all experimentation, that program introduced courses ranging from the sublime "Human Freedom and the Counterforces" to the seemingly ridiculous "Love in the Jungle." In fairness, all campuses have an ample supply of period pieces in their curriculums, but if programs and courses could resemble an attic, D&E would have some interesting, indeed bizarre, heirlooms to show off. However, it also displayed the courage to be different and thoughtful.

Camaraderie has been at the root of the faculty's ethos and so has academic freedom. Good-natured tolerance for academic proclivities has lent a great vitality to the D&E classroom. Indeed academic freedom, has also sheltered a few faculty members from the slings and arrows of uninformed opinions. William Phipps was roundly criticized by religious conservatives for his work *Was Jesus Married?* in 1969. Because the book was based in sound scholarship, the campus reception of Phipps' ideas was enthusiastic. Whatever else can be said, D&E has been a very "liberal" college in the best and oldest sense of that term.

But the most significant relationships have been those between students and faculty. Given its size, D&E has had a long tradition of professors knowing their students and establishing long relationships with them. James E. Allen, the fourth president of D&E, built up a strong following among students even as he steered the college through difficult times. Former students of Allen, in 1979, used expressions such as "great Virginia gentleman" and "real scholar" in their recollections of him. The man did not pander to gain popularity; he once gave his own son an "F" in Latin. In 1919, a school publication summed up his qualities by noting that he was a "gentleman of lofty ideals; a man of strong character," as well as being "cultured and broad-minded; a tireless worker." On the occasion of his son's birth in 1911, the students declared a holiday.

S. Benton Talbot, a long-time professor of biology who also served at one point as dean, is regarded to this day as a remarkable mentor among his former students. He began his career in 1926, serving until his death in 1958. He placed students into some of the finest medical schools in the country, including his alma mater Johns Hopkins, Georgetown University, the University of Virginia, and the University of Richmond. Other graduates of the program excelled academically, going to teach at prestigious universities and

Above: Dean of Women, Patty Petty, serves punch in Halliehurst
at a student reception, circa 1960s; Below: Typing class in the Commercial Classroom, circa 1918

Above: Drawing class with Charles Albert; Below: Library on the third floor of Liberal Arts Hall, 1935

Dr. Charles Albert

Jesse Reed

Lois Latham

receiving doctorates in biology. A colleague in the sciences, Charles Albert, served as academic dean from 1922 to 1935, acting president in 1935-36, and president from 1936 to 1939. A professor of physics, he was as effective in the classroom as in the presidential chair. Both Albert and Talbot epitomized the spirit of utilitarianism that has characterized D&E's history. Wearing many hats, they helped tackle the problems that came with managing a college while still pursuing their academic interests. Despite far-flung interests and concerns, Albert and Talbot presided over the sciences at D&E during one of its brightest periods.

Another faculty member who merged the culture of service in and outside the classroom was Fred Miller, a longtime professor of mathematics. He served as registrar and is regarded, in the words of Thomas Richard Ross, as "one of the ablest classroom instructors ever to teach at D&E." Others who combined classroom with community were Jesse Reed, a professor of art and history; James Welshonce, professor of economics; Sidney Tedford, director of choral

music; Barbara Tedford, professor of English; Ralph Booth, professor of chemistry; Claire Fiorentino in dramatic arts; and, of course, Raymond Purdum. All were loved by their students and reflected well on the institution.

D&E professors have been characterized by a willingness to advise students and to serve in whatever capacity they considered vital to the college. They rub shoulders with their charges and are available for personal consultation. This tradition was established early in the school's history and has continued, despite the tendency in some places to regard community service as secondary. The student, community, administration, and faculty are still regarded as a unit and all serve a common goal—the betterment of the college. Peter Okun of the English department calls it "lunch bucket" academics, a concept that certainly fits D&E. Whether it is a Habitat for Humanity project or a field trip to an art gallery, D&E professors have always been willing to take that extra step to enrich their students and give that most precious commodity—their time.

Dr. William Gartmann   *Claire Fiorentino*   *Dr. Margaret (Purdum) Goddin '50*

For many students, it is considered a highlight to be able to speak to their instructors informally. Gone are the pretenses of academic rank and hierarchical structure, and in their place is an atmosphere of congeniality. The professor seamlessly tries to connect with the student in a way that is not patronizing or forced. Sometimes the subject has little to do with a specific course but simply represents banter between two individuals. But it builds a bond of respect and affection, which gives a student a deeper understanding of the professor. In addition, it is a means to imparting why the faculty member chose the profession and why he/she has a passion for it.

Of course, D&E has had its share of professors who preened on their titles and dreamed they were at a more impersonal setting, but that has never been the norm. If anything, pretentiousness has long been frowned upon and has been regarded over time as inimical to what a D&E professor should be. And this does not refer to "teaching style." Some of the most effective professors have been lecturers, the often-derided "sage on the stage." Many are

able to form concepts and pictures in the heads of undergraduates that have inspired them to continue their studies after graduation. The secret, as they say, lies in the style in which a teacher approaches a student.

Embodying this mix of erudition and personal engagement was Lois Latham, an associate professor of English from 1955 to 1968. Latham, a graduate of the University of North Carolina-Chapel Hill, quickly impressed all with a keen intellect and flamboyant style. She made the subject of English literature come alive in the classroom. Her particular passion was Shakespeare—which she imparted with an intensity that brought her students with her. Some also remember her as an engaging and witty conversationalist who was always accessible to her students. Since the early 1980s, those characteristics have been remembered annually by the awarding of Davis & Elkins's highest award for teaching excellence and community service, which bears her name.

In the 1970s, few professors shone as brightly as Margaret (Purdum) Goddin and William Gartmann. Both were outstanding teachers in their fields—Goddin in English

Top: Religion Professor Dr. William Phipps lectures in class; lower left: Political Science Professor Dr. Dorothy Roberts; lower right: English Professor Dr. Phillips V. Brooks

and Gartmann in German—but they also epitomized the best in service. Goddin, the first woman to serve D&E as an academic dean, was a major force behind the innovative curriculum of the 1970s. She was lauded by Lloyd Averill, a particularly energetic dean at the time, as an "effective, patient, and efficient chairman" of the Educational Policies Committee that pushed through "all of the necessary curriculum changes and transitions on time and in good order." She was extraordinarily efficient and effective in forming programs—including Communications and later the Mentor Assisted Program, called MAP for short.

Gartmann left his mark as a prime mover of the Integrated Studies Program. He was highly regarded as an "idea" man who helped mastermind the reforms of the turbulent seventies. Gartmann's ideas were heavily weighed toward service and integrated studies. He also was a passionate advocate of academic reform. Gartmann retired in 1984 when it became clear that the integrated reform program was slowly being abandoned in favor of a more discipline-based core curriculum.

Gartmann's premature retirement robbed D&E of one of its more effective and imaginative workers. It also highlighted the tensions between innovation and traditions, academic achievement and community service. Too often, stereotypes have developed concerning the motives of those who hold different opinions and approaches concerning academic matters. Whispered views about "hidden agendas" and rude comments concerning more conservative academics have from time to time led to a winner-take-all approach in the development of the curriculum. Certainly, innovation can be a good thing, but it should not be developed at the expense of tried and true methods of the past. The lecturer, who has often been the target of advocates of the "learning approach" to education (as opposed to the "teaching approach"), can be a gem if enthusiastic and armed with current material. On the other hand, to be innovative does not mean that one has thrown all academic standards and, to the most mendacious academic traditionalist, all sanity to the winds. This either/or approach has often prevented the marriage of virtues. Learned lecturers can infuse passion in their messages while

the innovator can introduce new methods and ideas to the common goal of inspiring students to do better.

This academic tension has often been a force for good in a harmonious environment. Certainly, the St. Bartholomew's night approach of slaughtering—in this case, all innovators or all conservatives—is not preferable. Indeed, years later, even those on the side that may have won such confrontations sometimes moan that perhaps the balance was a trifle unsettled by going too far. It is the instructor who makes the course, and to whom all praise and criticism should be directed. The old method can be electrifying, provided that the professor is not addicted to yellowed notes and keeps up in his/her field. And, certainly, the enthusiasm and freshness of the academic prophet should never be crushed, for he/she too often represents the soul of the institution.

Creativity is not limited to the classroom or even to the academic program. D&E's theatre arts program has long been a source of pride for the campus community. Claire Fiorentino exemplified this tradition by participating in staging events for the college—even prior to becoming a faculty member. In October 1936, Fiorentino directed a pageant in honor of the visit of President Franklin D. Roosevelt during the Forest Festival. Entitled "A Legend of Peace," it reflected the pacifist sentiments of its day. She also was the architect of the May Day Fete. Her productions were community oriented, largely reflecting predominant opinion. She directed no fewer than ten Forest Festival performances. Her works were popular in the Elkins area. This popularity helped her secure a faculty position in 1944 when she was appointed assistant professor of dramatics and public speaking.

Fiorentino's taste ran to the contemporary classics and her plays were always immensely popular. Known as "Mrs. F" to her students, she is still remembered fondly. She staged the standards: *Our Town* in 1948; *The Glass Menagerie* and *The Philadelphia Story* in 1952-53; and light comedies such as *Kiss and Tell.* Her diligence and hard work earned her positions as chairman of her department and, in 1969, president of the West Virginia Intercollegiate Speech and Drama Association.

Fiorentino was succeeded in 1974 by Michael Pedretti,

*Top: J. Keith Hiser physics class, circa late 1950s; Below left; John Martin 1970s
chemistry class; Below right: Biology professor Dr. James Van Gundy
Opposite: professor of dramatics and public speaking Claire Fiorentino*

who was interested primarily in "movement theatre" or, in other words, mime. He established a good program and was known for a more daring approach to theatre. His plays were generally well received, and he was fully in step with the experimental tendencies of the time. During his tenure, he managed to coax faculty to participate in his productions. By the time he left D&E in 1983, his efforts in movement theatre were regionally recognized. He was succeeded as chairman of the theatre arts department by Terry Hayes who added to the program emphasis on technical theatre. Hayes struck a balance between the conservatism of Fiorentino and the progressive ideas of Pedretti.

Music has also enjoyed considerable success at D&E with its emphasis on performance, from an emphasis on sacred a capella music under the direction of Sidney Tedford in the 1960s and 1970s, to the flashy "Jazz Singers" under Richard Kadel in the 1980s, to the more academic approach to performance and music education under Robert Psurny today.

Introducing sophisticated arrangements and a scholarly approach to choir, the music department certainly cannot be accused of pandering to popular taste.

Art has also undergone a shift. Jesse Reed, like Fiorentino, was conservative in his approach to art, preferring portraits and landscapes. In recent years, social abstraction has been vigorously introduced. All of the fine arts have demonstrated this ability to change and embrace the new when the times have called for it.

One successful arts program is not even a part of the college's academic offerings. The Augusta Heritage Center has been a strong program since its founding in 1972 as a community initiative. It became a unit of the college in 1981. Part of, in one reporter's words, a "grassroots movement to preserve and promulgate Appalachian Folk Arts," Augusta partially reflected a movement to rediscover tradition. The original suggestion for the program came from Mrs. W.R. Cromwell and Jesse Reed. It took the prodigious talents of

Associate Professor of English Donald Bloom and his students "take it outside" on the flagstones in front of Albert Hall.

Top: "And All That Jazz", with director Richard Kadel (right front), circa early 1980s
Bottom: Augusta Heritage Center Spring Dulcimer Week 2004

Margaret Goddin to convert the concept into a working idea.

In its early years, it concentrated primarily on a narrow Appalachian theme. However, in the 1980s, traditional arts would be given a far more expanded dimension.

Margo Blevin has directed the program from the 1980s to the present. Under her tutelage, Augusta expanded to include other traditional cultures and weave them seamlessly into the program. Emphasis on Irish, Cajun, and African-American blues were added to the general Appalachian theme. The courses attracted top-notch instructors who added much to the summers at D&E. One writer called Irish Week a "Who's Who in Celtic Music." Dewey Balfa and others capped off Cajun Week, while Nat Reese highlighted Blues. Renowned fiddlers Woody Simmons and Melvin Wine were fixtures at Augusta and John Hartford headlined, as well. Undergirding the whole program was the understanding that all traditional cultures have much in common with other folk genres. What took root in the bogs of Louisiana or in Ireland, or perhaps in

St. Louis and Chicago, had a great deal to do with West Virginia and its Appalachian heritage. This, perhaps, is Blevin's greatest accomplishment—bringing these diverse artistic expressions together in a lively celebration of heritage arts.

Not that Appalachian culture has received short shift in this period. On the contrary, Gerry Milnes, a first rate fiddler and folklorist, is on hand to certify authenticity and inter-connections between cultures. Author of a number of noted works, Milnes recognizes, as does Blevin, the interconnection between seemingly dissimilar cultures. The summer seminars were described by a *New York Times* correspondent as an "exhausting experience—by week's end," noting that "the diehards walk around in a glassy-eyed stupor, resigned to minimal rest—until they return home." But he noted that it was "fulfilling to participate" and, for him, it was apparently a lot of fun. The reporter stated that Augusta was so absorbing that after a few days, despite the intense study, "it felt entirely natural to go walking after midnight strumming a guitar and

Above: Librarian Mary Margaret Carroll Woodward '44;
Lower left: campus mail carrier Gerald "Jerry" Morrison; Lower right: Vernie Roy, longtime alumni office secretary
Opposite: Anna J. Parmesano '19, who served forty-four years as secretary to the president,
from 1920 to 1964, receives a gift from Hank Henry, director of alumni, upon her retirement

looking for a jam session." Again, D&E adheres to the dictum that formal schooling should not always interfere with your education. Augusta adds this dimension, with an intensity and a color all its own.

Augusta Heritage Center is certainly not the only ancillary group that contributes to the college. Upward Bound, a federally-funded program housed on the D&E campus, works throughout the year with West Virginia high school students to prepare them to be successful in college and in life. The summer sessions, or the bridge program, get recent high school graduates off to a proper start with introductory courses. Often these students do not attend D&E in the fall; however, the college provides instruction for these aspiring scholars. Its counterpart, Veterans Upward Bound, also housed on the D&E campus, helps veterans retool educationally for the demands of the workplace. Both of these programs offer valuable services to the citizens of Randolph County and the region and, by doing so, connect the college to the larger community.

Certainly, the local community has enriched the college in countless ways. For example, College Aid provides "a social link of friendship between the people of Elkins and the Davis & Elkins College faculty and their families." Organized in 1935, its first president was Mrs. W.E. Baker and it began its work to help the college in whatever capacity it could. It has also provided a forum for Davis & Elkins faculty to present ideas and, in some cases, entertainment.

The school would certainly be a less effective institution if it were not for those members of the support staff. I can attest to the secretarial staff—Jean Jones, Sharon White, Carolyn Church, Robin Price, and Ann Harris—who have been immensely helpful to me over the years. Some—Jones and Price—have helped mightily in the preparation of this work. All contribute a huge service to the college. White often reminds forgetful professors that meetings are at hand; Church makes sure that students learn "the ropes" in their first few days at D&E. All have been pearls beyond price and deserve special recognition. The performance of these and many other staff members represents a continuation of an old tradition of going that extra mile for the progress of D&E.

Perhaps the greatest secretary in Davis & Elkins's history was Anna J. Parmesano, who served forty-four years as secretary to the president, from 1920 to 1964. Charles Albert lauded her for having a "splendid attitude" for providing "highly efficient service" and projecting a "kindly spirit" which "endeared her to all." Mabel (Van Scoy) Phanes provided outstanding support to three deans. Also, Beth (Guye) Kittle served President Hermanson well as an academic secretary and later became director of alumni relations. Price, as well, has done a stellar job as assistant to Presidents MacConkey and Mann.

Another employee of note was Stephen "Steve" Martin who served D&E as a custodian for thirty-three years, from 1932 to 1965. And until his retirement, Gerald "Jerry" Morrison was the fondly regarded campus postman. Cheerful and ever faithful to D&E, he was a reassuring presence for lonely students and an efficient deliverer of packages. He had a good sense of humor and added a bright touch on otherwise dreary days. Jan Chadwick, Coordinator of Conference Services and wife of political science professor Tom Chadwick, personified the shared values of service before self until her untimely death in 1998.

The library staff has for years heroically acquired materials for faculty members and students alike. Their service to the institution is immeasurable, despite short budgets and strained conditions. Indeed, their heroics in inter-library loan or helping one fumble through microfilm are not to be underestimated. For a historian, whose first line of advance is the librarian and archivist, it would be rather ungrateful not to salute the librarians. From Virgie Harris to Mary Margaret Woodward to Ellis Hodgin, the tradition of excellence continues.

However, one member of the D&E family deserves special note. He is often seen plowing snow early in the mornings and on weekends, motivated always by his interest in the safety and beauty of the campus. Thomas "Tom" Shockey is a great representative of the spirit that Professor Stary spoke of so eloquently in 1944. As a member of the buildings and grounds staff at D&E, he represents a most noble unselfishness that would be good to dwell on. Shockey personifies the dedication of a community to the betterment of D&E College. It is, indeed, a spirit which all would be encouraged to catch.

*Faculty at commencement, President Dr. R.T.L. Liston, Harry E. Whetsell, Dr. Thomas F. Marshall,
Dr. Raymond B. Purdum, Dr. S. Benton Talbot and Virgie Harris, circa 1941*

Student Life

Every year they come from different states and various backgrounds. Some are local, living short distances away. Arriving on the campus at Davis & Elkins College, freshmen begin an odyssey that will lead to new adventures and experiences. Gathering at their residence halls, meeting with their academic advisors to plan a schedule, and making friends quickly, the life of a first-year student begins to take shape on opening day. When they come, they behold a beautiful campus and gaze on terrain as awe inspiring as any in the world. At the beginning most are novices; at the end many are adults. Unknown to many when they first set foot on the campus are the relationships they will build in the years ahead. Friends of a lifetime, and perhaps even a spouse, await them, as well as academic and social skills that can literally change the course of their lives.

Opposite: 1984 Miss D&E Sherri Coleman and Mr. Senator Rick Barlow

For one hundred years Davis & Elkins has welcomed these students. Over the years, classes have brought their own distinctive styles. Some of the earlier students came in high collars; during the 1920s and 1930s they donned letterman sweaters. Up until the 1970s, freshmen wore beanies. After World War II, some arrived with the seriousness that comes from military service during wartime. Over time, the campus has undergone fashion transformations—pleated skirts, saddle shoes, Bass Weejuns, hiking boots, sweater sets, and some in the uniform of Air Force Reserve cadets. By the 1970s, chinos, Levis, parkas, and ponchos replaced the button-down style of the 1960s. Morphed together, the D&E student resembles a relatively conservative person with an openness to experimentation. More than faculty, staff, or administration, the students stand out as the most important group. It is their style, brash and studious, that has changed the school.

Over the decades, the students led the way in shaping the college. They have tended to express common complaints. They decry the cafeteria food—all the while gaining weight from consumption of it. Many groused that certain interests were not represented in the curriculum. Sometimes the students have directed criticism at the administration and faculty. But they have also shared enthusiasm for a college that has engaged their curiosity and spurred them to higher achievement. On the whole, the D&E students have been far more positive than negative.

In the college's earlier years, D&E produced students who were respectful towards authority. They referred affectionately to "the Prexy"—the President—and celebrated the achievements of the athletic department. Football mania took hold in the 1920s and 1930s, as it did on many college campuses. These were the years of the BMOC—Big Man on Campus—the role model which was held up for others to emulate. Press Maravich, the basketball star, was also elected president of the student body in 1940. Most were unquestioning of the government. There was very little outcry for

"America First" on the eve of World War II. When President Franklin D. Roosevelt signed the Selective Service Act in September 1940, D&E students and some faculty eagerly trooped to the colors. Thirty-eight students and four professors registered for the draft. A campus poll showed overwhelming support, better than 3-1 favoring the law.

During World War II, as we have seen, D&E was converted into a military training facility. After the war, veterans streamed onto campus, quite serious about their education. The experiences of Tarawa, Okinawa, Normandy, the Bulge, and air combat in the Pacific and over Europe did not orient these students toward having a "hell of a time." The campus had a military feel to it. Its promotion campaign in 1944, "Forward-at-Forty," sported trainees and cadets marching on campus. The students of the late 1940s were, by and large, all business. Veterans were eager to get out, not stick around. Some lived in military-style accommodations in Quonset huts. The ROTC band often supplied music—at one point unintentionally ruffling a faculty member's feathers. (A certain language professor—who happened to be from Georgia—took exception to the band's rendition of "Marching Through Georgia" in 1957, leaving a concert in a huff.)

Accordingly, given this atmosphere of earnestness and ramrod-straight demeanor, the campus was predictably conservative. This was not much of a stretch from previous years. Halliehurst, which in this period was a women's residence hall, had a strict set of rules in the early 1940s. "Study hours" were set from 7:30 to 10:30 every night, without exception. Women were prohibited from venturing into Elkins without an escort. From Wednesday to Saturday their rooms underwent thorough inspection. If you were an upperclassman, you were given certain privileges only if you had an overall average of at least a B. Religious services on Sunday were mandatory.

Although frivolity was encouraged, it was decidedly organized. The May festival, which extended into the 1960s,

*Students socialize in the college snackbar, located in a World War II-era
army surplus building that stood on the current site of Randolph Hall*

remained the highlight of the year. At that time, students attended the ball well decked out in their finery—men in tuxedos, women in evening gowns. The Queen of the May Fete and her escort marched through a forest of sabers all held up by crisply-attired cadets. The 1940s and 1950s marked the high point of organizations at D&E—and in the United States, for that matter. The college had Beta Alpha Beta, a business fraternity; Chi Beta Phi; Zeta Sigma; the Student Christian Organization; the Playcrafters, led by Fiorentino; the Varsity Club; and the Women's Athletic Association, which revived the May Fete in 1946. Other organizations reflected the changes and interests of the postwar era. Predictably there was a Veterans Club, an International Relations Club, Phi Alpha Theta, the Golden Circle, the Golden Chain, Sigma Tau Delta, and the Book Club.

Social fraternities also flourished during the era. In 1951, three national fraternities called D&E home. Alpha Sigma Phi, Sigma Phi Epsilon, and Tau Kappa Epsilon were joined by three sororities—Chi Omega, Phi Mu, and Pi Beta Phi. The entertainments revolved around sports and very polite

socials. Alcohol was prohibited on campus, and students were contented with restrained amusements.

Of course, things could get out of hand from time to time. In November 1956, a group of West Virginia Wesleyan students led a "raid" on Halliehurst Hall. This was ostensibly done in retaliation for an attempt by Davis & Elkins students to do the same to a Wesleyan women's domicile. Despite the fact that the local authorities and the Inter-Mountain were not amused, the students saw it as great fun. One male student exulted, "D&E has finally become a full-fledged college. The raids are great for school spirit."

It was all in the spirit of the times—the era of housemothers and housefathers; the pinnacle of *in loco parentis* when the college could act as parents to students. One observer called the atmosphere "authoritarian." Very little in the way of political activism marked the activity of students. When Adlai Stevenson, the Democratic nominee for president in 1956, visited D&E, he was warmly greeted. Even if some students "liked Ike," they nevertheless greeted all politely and with respect. Foreign affairs were rarely subjected to a critical eye.

LEOLA CHENEY   RALPH FINLEY   M. LEIGHTY   PAUL OSBORNE
CAPTAIN
DAVIS AND ELKINS

Above: …and the correct answer is…team from D&E on a nationally televised
quiz show, the General Electric College Bowl, May 24, 1970
Opposite: 1941 May Queen Aileen Marteney (Phares) '42 with retiring queen, Leah Fitzwater (Richards) '41 as her maid

Top: 1960 graduating class; Opposite below: Science Hall (now Albert Hall) burns after it was struck by lightning on May 22, 1956, during finals week; Below left: Highlanders lead the commencement procession; Below right: commencement procession around the chapel

Indeed, Air Force ROTC flourished during the era, and the campus had a military air to it. The mainstream was the norm, and students were encouraged to be diligent and, for the most part, uncritical.

Yet this era up to 1970 produced some superb graduates. Lawyers, scientists, physicians, and college professors were produced from their ranks. Michael DiMario, class of 1960, later became the United States Printer. Fred Fox, 1960, and Charles Clevert, 1969, donned judicial robes. Andy Fry, 1969, later earned a Ph.D. in history and currently serves as Distinguished Professor of History at the University of Nevada at Las Vegas. Syngman Rhee, 1957, became an ordained Presbyterian minister, professor at Union Theological Seminary, and in 2000 was elected moderator of the Presbyterian Church (USA).

S. Benton Talbot, along with Charles Albert, prepared students in abundance for entrance to medical schools. They also aided students such as Mohsen Ziai, an Iranian who arrived in 1946 and found that D&E was a convivial place eager to help a lonely stranger. He later became a medical doctor, educator, and a high official in the health administration of the last Shah of Iran. Many aspiring students found their way into medicine and public health in the postwar period.

The late 1960s saw the first inklings of change. D&E had some student activism; three students marched for voting rights for African Americans at Selma, Alabama, in 1965, but more typically it was mainstream protest. The Vietnam War did not receive organized student dissent until 1969. Indeed, at the beginning of escalation in Vietnam, the students clearly supported the position of President Lyndon B. Johnson. A poll for *The Senator* in October 1965 showed backing for the conflict. The editor, Elizabeth Leahy, described the war as a "necessary evil which must be engaged in."

Mind you, this was a position a bit to the right of some D&E faculty members. William Phipps and James Dow were remarkably perceptive and far out in front of the student

Vice President Hubert H. Humphrey, center, visited the college in October 1966
To Humphrey's left is Davis & Elkins President Gordon E. Hermanson, Mrs. Hermanson is over Humphrey's right shoulder

Clockwise from upper right: David Sutton, 1976;
Madras madness, 1965; Dorm life 1948, Dorm room, 1976

body. "I lament that we did not learn from the French," opined Phipps, "the futility of fighting to protect the Vietnamese from domination by Communist leadership...." Dow went Phipps one better and anticipated events ten years later, stating that "unless we are prepared to fight a major war of extermination, we shall eventually have to come to terms with what those guerrillas call communism...."

While other campuses joined in protesting the war, D&E remained sedate. When Vice President Hubert H. Humphrey visited the college in October 1966, he was greeted with warmth and enthusiasm. When college students were needed to provide support for the war, Davis & Elkins was one that was selected to send a delegation to Washington. In May 1967, a group of students, led by Student Body President Robert Baird, met with John P. Roche to discuss the war. Roche, who was a special assistant specifically employed to deal with anti-war groups, was eager to showcase a group of mid-American students that supported the war. Davis & Elkins received an invitation because it was passive, not because of a raucous reputation. After all, the administration was under siege in 1967 and desired to show another face of public opinion.

Change did not begin to sweep over D&E until the 1970s. There were exceptions, with students actively participating in Vietnam Moratorium activities on October 15, 1969. *The Senator* contained no articles but was festooned with peace symbols and biblical quotations. But all of it reflected what Thomas Richard Ross called a "well-behaved" student body. Although there were anti-Vietnam protests, certainly the campus had no groups comparable to the Students for a Democratic Society.

After the Kent State incident on May 4, 1970, in which four students were killed by Ohio National Guardsmen, there was little reaction on campus. Neighboring colleges and universities demonstrated, but not D&E. Some students went to Washington, D.C., to register their disapproval with the Nixon administration for its invasion of Cambodia, the incident that had prompted the Kent State disturbances. However, D&E dissenters remained too small a group to make much impact on campus. Indeed, in May 1970, more students were enthralled by an appearance of a team from D&E on a national television quiz show, the General Electric College Bowl.

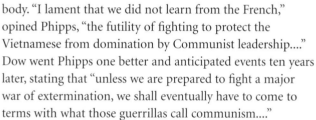

D&E "women" have always been known for their shapely legs.

Representatives of the North Central Association of Colleges and Schools noticed during their visit in 1970 that the campus seemed to have little in the way of campus activism. One student leader meeting with the delegations told them that "apathy certainly has to be spelled with capital letters" on campus. They noticed that the student body was "overall more conservative in manners and style than is true at some other colleges." They also noted the preponderance and dominance of the fraternities, asserting that "a good deal of the social life on campus is organized."

As has been noted, D&E administration and faculty attempted to infuse a sense of social responsibility in the 1970s by designing a new curriculum. One of the innovations was the winter session that ran for six weeks in 1970. This session was highlighted by field trips, including one to Harlem in New York City where students worked with welfare agencies, and by special courses including one on international relations taught by a guest lecturer, Dr. L.N. Palar, an Indonesian scholar and politician. The early attempts at reinvigorating campus life seemed to be successful.

The integrated studies program, or "liberated life sequence" also attempted to challenge students to engage social issues. The freshman course, "Human Freedom and the Counterforces" was broken up into units: "World Cultures," "Comparative Ideas," and the capstone, "The Future." Practica in business and psychology offered, in the jargon of the day, "hands-on" experiences.

Foreign travel was also encouraged. Professors Phillips V. Brooks and Jesse Reed regularly accompanied students to London. Brooks, as well, planned trips to the Shakespeare festival in Stratford, Ontario. Georgina Vazquez and Jean Minnick traveled with students to the Caribbean.

Environmentalism received a boost with the development of an interdisciplinary major in ecology and environmental

Above: The Ice House, circa 1970s
Overleaf: Campus and town, 1957

studies by Professor William Tolstead. Other programs such as the newly organized "Orientation in the Woods," later "Woods Orientation," caught the "Mother Earth" sentiments of the early 1970s. Also interesting was a winter course developed by Brooks and librarian Douglas Oleson which emphasized surviving for three weeks on Spruce Knob. Mary Ellen Schubert, a student who experienced this course in 1976, remembered that it was exhilarating to wake up with six inches of snow at the flap of the tent. In its inaugural year in 1972, the Spruce Knob survival course gained the attention of the *Washington Post.*

For the first half of the 1970s, this attempt to infuse a new sense of enthusiasm for experiential education appeared to succeed. But by decade's end, North Central representatives noted that many students resented the curriculum. In the end, the revolution had been imposed by above, and, by the 1980s, most of the spirit of experimentation had dissipated.

The 1960s, however, had brought forth a more permanent revolution—one more of a social than of a pedagogical or political variety. In the spring of 1969, at the board of trustees meeting, a rebellion of a sort took place. With "in loco parentis" ruled unconstitutional by the Supreme Court in 1968, students were eager to make reforms. Rules prohibiting alcohol use, residence hall restrictions in regard to women, and other controls were denounced by students as being woefully out of step with the spirit of the age. They got results, having obtained 645 student signatures, and, in short order, the last vestiges of *in loco parentis* were gone. By October 1969, the board went further and voted to "temporarily cancel the convocation and worship program." The emphasis was on student "choices" and the board dutifully complied.

This was the age of change—pass/fail courses, D-F stipulations, and generally a de-emphasis on authority or elitism. By 1974, the last reminder of the late 1940s and 1950s was removed. The Air Force ROTC program, which, due to Vietnam, had been declining for years, was deactivated.

The "Union of Cross and Sword", the "old morality," was now being replaced by the "Age of Aquarius"—academic experimentation.

Perhaps the greatest expression of the new spirit of liberation at the campus was the organization of a campus pub in 1969. The "Ice House," which was established as an attempt to keep students on campus, was a declaration of independence of sorts from the old rules. By 1970-71, another dagger was placed in the heart of any blue-nosed puritan who may have objected to change. The board of trustees voted to "permit beer on the campus on a trial basis during the remainder of the academic year." Good God—the red cap of liberty was now donned with a Budweiser label firmly attached.

The chairman of the board of trustees, one Dr. R.A. Pfrangle, explained to those members of the clergy who may have been offended that the college had no choice but to bow to realities. One telling passage declared that D&E students "like students everywhere...are extremely sensitive to the question of whether they are being treated as children or adults." He asserted that "they [students] are extremely resentful of what they regard as the hypocrisy of adults who would impose upon students standards of behavior that are not generally observed in the adult world, even within the membership of our churches."

In a very large respect, the Ice House has stood as a monument to the reforms of that era. A charming structure, it has been a social hub of the campus for better than thirty years. For many students, the place marked a period of social maturity and growth. A *New York Times* correspondent, John Milward, writing about Augusta in 1993, dubbed the Ice House a "funky beer hall." Certainly, in 1969, it was a bit of a "funky" surprise to the denizens of the old Davis & Elkins, with their military style and old-time Presbyterianism. By 1972, you had a functioning Ice House on campus; a new "space age" chapel, as it was dubbed; liberalized campus rules; and a trendy curriculum.

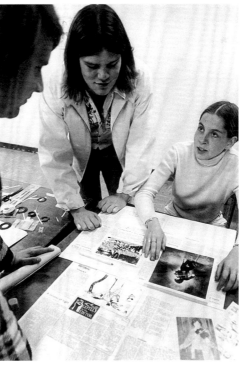

Top: 1964 Student Council pictured in the Randolph County Courthouse;
Below left: Gail Bartow, Susie Davis, Marsha Thompson and Jarrell Simmons enjoy Roaring Twenties Night in 1970;
Below right: Senator *editor Barbara Porter (right), Pat Ferguson and an unidentified staffer review pasteups in 1976.*

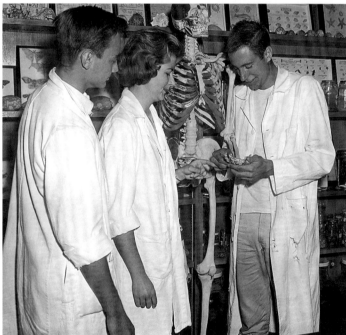

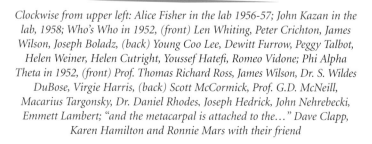

Clockwise from upper left: Alice Fisher in the lab 1956-57; John Kazan in the lab, 1958; Who's Who in 1952, (front) Len Whiting, Peter Crichton, James Wilson, Joseph Boladz, (back) Young Coo Lee, Dewitt Furrow, Peggy Talbot, Helen Weiner, Helen Cutright, Youssef Hatefi, Romeo Vidone; Phi Alpha Theta in 1952, (front) Prof. Thomas Richard Ross, James Wilson, Dr. S. Wildes DuBose, Virgie Harris, (back) Scott McCormick, Prof. G.D. McNeill, Macarius Targonsky, Dr. Daniel Rhodes, Joseph Hedrick, John Nehrebecki, Emmett Lambert; "and the metacarpal is attached to the…" Dave Clapp, Karen Hamilton and Ronnie Mars with their friend

*Clockwise from upper left: TKE Car Bash, 1962; Language Lab;
Production of* The Prime of Miss Jean Brodie *1987; Production
of* Turn Back-Oh-Man *with Bruce Fleshman, John Sarcona,
Jonesy Maxon, Jeff Anderson and Mike Gelber, 1978;
Carl "Chuck" Yeager '76 spinning vinyl on WCDE*

Students in the 1970s were primarily concerned with individual expression, preferring to gain the professor's ear rather than expertise. Yet, the era is memorable for its sense of freedom. Long hair for men and blue jeans for both sexes all represented a casual approach. The spit and polish elegance of an older era was replaced with a come-as-you-are attitude. Photographs from that period emanate a flash-and-dash demeanor on the part of students. Generally, they were a happy lot, content with themselves and comfortable with their friends.

Yet the academic experiment designed to forge a student body more concerned with the outside world came up short. By the 1980s, the experiment with swinging Calvinism produced somewhat of a hangover. The liberalization of campus life remained, if not the liberal spirit of integrated studies. The late 1980s saw the return of a more traditional curriculum, but no return of a traditional campus. Instead, student life had a fraternity and sorority feel with a considerable influence from the counterculture. In 1989, the North Central team found that student activities concentrated on "beer and band parties."

Of course, Davis & Elkins was not alone in this trend. The restlessness of the 1960s and 1970s gave way to a hedonism in the 1980s. Student Life directors attempted to put the genie back into the bottle in the early 1990s—trying to enforce rules which had not been vigorously pressed since the 1970s. Sometimes the attempts were comic. At one Déjà vu celebration, fearing that students were drinking too much, Student Life came up with a means to control it: provide beer and plenty of it—in fact, twenty kegs worth. It was, by every accounting, a wild affair. Meanwhile, states changed their drinking age—in West Virginia's case, from 19 to 21. This naturally placed pressure on the Ice House to police their customers to prevent underage drinking.

Despite the complaint that D&E had become too much of

a "party school," the administration had to shoulder some of the blame. During the late 1980s and early 1990s, activism was discouraged. This extended to the newly improved convocations that were reinstated in the mid-eighties. When Karl Bermann, a highly regarded author of a book on Central America, arrived on campus and lambasted U.S. policy toward Nicaragua, the academic dean demanded equal time for the government. There was a general ban on political posters, for Democrats and Republicans, during the 1988 campaign. Not willing to allow substantive activity, they left the students little option but to seek other amusements.

There were some bright moments—mostly supplied by the editorial staff of *The Senator*. Tom Van Sant and Larry Smith revived the newspaper and made it a force on campus. Particularly, Smith focused on larger issues rather than campus concerns. Indeed, he offered syndicated columns from well-known commentators that generated interest in the community. In fact, the paper was sold off campus and did a brisk business. In 1988, it received recognition as an outstanding campus paper from the West Virginia Press Association.

But the era was not dull. Students were high-spirited and colorful. Many an accomplished graduate came from the late 1980s and 1990s—lawyers, businessmen, Peace Corps volunteers, missionaries, and physicians came out of this period. One graduate, Gary Gregg, 1990, went on to obtain a Ph.D. in political science at Miami University, Ohio, and now holds an endowed chair at the University of Louisville. Political activity was evident despite attempts to discourage it. It was edgy, interesting, and, more importantly, it came with no prompting from above. Yet, it was mixed with a heavy dose of hedonism. Fraternity row met Jerry Garcia, and it provided a good match.

Opposite: Spirited game of frisbee in front of Liberal Arts Hall.

Above: "Me da Queen" and "her" royal court clean-up on a Homecoming float;
Below: Pinball Wizards circa 1970s

Above: 1960s Alpha Sigma Phi Flintstone party
Below: Tug-of-war

By the mid-1990s, the best efforts of reformers began to bear fruit. The emphasis was on non-controversial events and planned fun. Doubtless some of the excesses of the era needed to be curtailed; a certain dullness settled over campus life. Yet, students still went to classes and struck up relationships that lasted for years to come. Throughout, D&E remained a safe campus—which has always been a hallmark.

It is well to remember that the student is truly the life blood of the institution, and almost exclusively so in regard to social activities. Indeed, D&E students have been, in the main, responsible while maintaining their individuality. The problem of maintaining an active campus lies somewhere between tradition and experimentation. To micro-manage students, as many have found to their displeasure, is virtually impossible.

The best way to influence students is to show guidance, to urge restraint, and to encourage interest in things outside the campus. However, to suppress imagination or expression is to risk turning the institution into a dull diploma-granting factory. To superimpose one's own taste on students is to risk the numbing puritanism of an earlier age and the life-suppressing political correctness of a later period. Perhaps Dr. Pfrangle had it right when, speaking of alcohol in the 1970s, he stated that "college officials acknowledge that it would be almost impossible to enforce the present rules effectively without transforming the campus into a kind of police state." Indeed, the best route is to trust the student and allow the campus to blossom in a way that encourages the "better angels" to come forth.

Above: October 1998 – Sigma Phi Epsilon Fun Day during Family Weekend
Opposite: Greg Mitchell '95, Hilary Cedarberg '93 and James Sweeney '94

Epilogue

Thomas Richard Ross, in his seventy-five year history of Davis & Elkins, chose to end his work with these words:

D&E had had her full share of failures and disappointments, but her achievements far outweighed her shortcomings. Thus, as those who loved "the little College on the Hill" looked forward to the future they might well have thought of the Latin motto of an old Presbyterian clan in Scotland: Spem successus alit (Success nourishes hope!).

Certainly this applies as much to the period since 1980, when Ross penned these final sentences, as it did to the time prior. Like many church-related institutions, D&E over time has changed vastly its way of preparing its students for life. Yet, remarkably, it has remained faithful to its goals of providing a quality education not only for West Virginians, but for all. Over the years, many a fine scholar has inspired students to go on to greater heights and to appreciate the finer points of inquiry and critical thinking. For an institution that has existed on a modest endowment, this has been no mean feat.

And money has been at the heart of it. The football program could not be sustained without adequate funds. Even some of the curriculum reforms of the 1970s foundered on the rocks of penury. Faculty members have often "gone without" to help sustain the college. Unfortunately, some have left as a result. Yet, D&E has been a hothouse of new ideas and programs. More than most of its competitors, D&E has always been filled with colorful characters and innovative minds. It has also shown the will to change and to absorb the shock of the new.

It is because of its history and not despite it that Davis & Elkins faces the future with confidence. During good and bad times, the college has strived to meet its obligations to the students and to the community. Certainly, history has demonstrated that D&E, over one hundred years, can weather crises and adapt to changing conditions.

From its earlier days, when survival was questionable, to the present, Davis & Elkins has modified its mission many times over. In the 1920s and 1930s, the college offered a plethora of "practical" courses to see it through the bad times. Under President Purdum, the emphasis on veterans allowed the institution to flourish. In the late 1950s to 1969, Davis & Elkins appeared to reach what many had dreamed of in previous years. It became a solid and accomplished liberal arts college. Yet, in the 1970s, in response to cries for "relevant" courses and programs, it changed again to an experiential model. By the late 1980s, it became a "comprehensive liberal arts college" which split the difference between the liberal arts and a vocational professional curriculum.

It has been a journey of the survivor who, at times, prospers and then has to adjust the course of action. However, on the trip, the institution gradually begins to create new ways of improving. D&E's innovative approaches, such as the integrated studies of the 1970s, did receive wide praise. In time, however, the zeal for self-discovery and inquiry gave way to the search for a diploma. In this respect, D&E is no different from other colleges and universities.

But what shines through from 1904 to 2004 is the devotion to the institution from every strata of the college during its history. Presidents, professors, and staff have all broken bread together and spoken to each other in hallways and in stairwells. All have borne the burdens of economic crisis; some in the 1930s eschewed paychecks, and others volunteered their services. All would embrace the spirit of Daniel Webster when arguing that Dartmouth keep its original charter rather than be absorbed by the State of New Hampshire. "It is, sir," intoned Webster, "a small college and yet there are those who love it."

The lack of pretension at the college has been a saving grace during anxious times. It is a spirit seen every year during the Woods Orientation when professors meet students in an exposed and vulnerable setting. It is true at the end-of-the-year picnics and in the various settings that bring the D&E community together. The "Boar's Head" dinner in years past evoked the same spirit of oneness. It also stressed an egalitarian atmosphere.

Charles Albert, in a *Brief History of Davis & Elkins College* compiled in 1965, related a story—from the college's earliest days—of a maintenance man named Dick Barry. At Christmas time, through no initiative except his own, he would decorate the second floor of the Science Hall. Using greenery from West Virginia and some "imported...from other southern states," he added a bit of cheer every Christmas. Just before the holiday vacation, he would arrange logs to provide seats between Liberal Arts and the then Science Hall, and would place a very large log in the center—the Yule log. He kept the log burning throughout the day and the night. He then placed a string of Christmas bells and sleigh bells on a rope so students could ring them. Barry did this with love and asked for little compensation except the joy it brought the students.

This spirit of love does not come naturally, but only after years of nurturing. It has survived a few pompous and preening academics and college bureaucrats. Yet, it is a feeling that has inspired many a graduate to give back

much to the institution. William "Bill" Robbins, class of 1956, recently provided a substantial gift to D&E. He was quiet, modest, and unassuming, giving as a labor of love rather than obligation. He gave out of the "spirit" that Georgiana Stary described in 1944—out of hope and optimism, or as Stary put it, "While the halls echoed their emptiness, this faculty talked of building up departments, of adding staff, books [and] buildings." Despite her doubts, she found "these were not idle dreams, but down to earth plans calling for consecration and hard work." Robbins's generous gifts, as well as his unassuming air, capture perfectly what Stary referred to as the "spirit" of D&E.

Davis & Elkins proudly enters its second century committed to improvement, but also to never forgetting the unpretentious style of the past. It remembers well the humanity of everyone who works and strives on its campus. We would be well to remember William Faulkner's address to the Nobel Committee, in which he said that the individual...

is immortal, not because he alone among creatures has an inexhaustible voice, but because he has a soul, a spirit capable of compassion and sacrifice and endurance. The poet's, the writer's duty is to write about these things. It is his privilege to help man endure by lifting his heart, by reminding him of the courage and honor and hope and pride and compassion and pity and sacrifice which have been the glory of his past. The poet's voice need not merely be the record of man, it can be one of the props, the pillars to help him endure and prevail.

Let us hope that Davis & Elkins, in the future, holds to Faulkner's advice as it continues to shape its mission.

Selected Bibliography

Clagg, Sam. *The Cam Henderson Story: His Life and Times.* Parsons, WV: McClain Printing Company, 1981.

Kennedy, David. *Freedom From Fear.* New York: Oxford University Press, 1999.

Morris, Edmund. *Theodore Rex: The Presidency of Theodore Roosevelt.* New York: Modern Library, 2002.

Pringle, Henry. *Theodore Roosevelt: A Biography.* New York: Harcourt Brace, 1931.

Ross, Thomas Richard. *Davis & Elkins College: The Diamond Jubilee History.* Parsons, WV: McClain Printing Company, 1980.

Ross, Thomas Richard. *Henry Gassaway Davis: An Old-Fashioned Biography.* Parsons, WV: McClain Printing Company, 1994.

Summers, Mark Wahlgren. *Rum Romanism and Rebellion: The Making of the President 1884.* Chapel Hill, NC: University of North Carolina Press, 2000.

Whetsell, Robert C. *Elkins, West Virginia: The Metropolis Revisited.* Parsons, WV: McClain Printing Company, 1994.

Williams, John Alexander. *West Virginia and the Captains of Industry.* Morgantown, WV: West Virginia University Library, 1976.

Documents:

North Central Association of Colleges and Schools, Evaluation Team Reports. Dec. 1959

North Central Association of Colleges and Schools, Evaluation Team Reports. April 20-21, 1970

North Central Association of Colleges and Schools, Evaluation Team Reports. April 21-23, 1980

North Central Association of Colleges and Schools, Evaluation Team Reports. Nov. 13-15, 1989

North Central Association of Colleges and Schools, Evaluation Team Reports. March 27, 2000

Unpublished Manuscripts:

Albert, Charles E. *A Brief History of Davis & Elkins College.*

Gear, Felix P. *Davis & Elkins College As I Knew It: 1920-1923.*

Stary, Georgiana. *Reminiscences of a College Professor.* Prepared as part of the fiftieth anniversary celebration materials.

Articles

Kerry L. Bryan. "*The Augusta Experience.*" Irish Edition, Vol XXI No 9, Sept. 2001.

John Milward. "*Playing the Blues in West Virginia.*" *New York Times,* May 9, 1993.

Acknowledgements

Research, editing, photography, and creative direction provided by the Davis & Elkins College Centennial Publications Committee:

Patricia Schumann, Chair
Ellis Hodgin
Beth Guye Kittle
G. Thomas Mann
Peter Okun
Thomas Richard Ross
Carol Schuler
Karen Wilmoth

Other assistance provided by:

Wendy Cunningham
Jean Jones
Robin Price
Lisa Senic

Photo Credits:

Kevin Cooke, Brent Kepner, Charles Potter, STAMATS Communications, Inc. The many anonymous photographers whose pictures were found in our archives or submitted by alumni and friends of the College.

CHAP
WAGNER
'94